# Mental Models

*The Complete Guide to Learn the Fundamentals of Mental Training and Improve Focus and Self-Discipline.*

**By**

**Brandon Dark**

# Table of Contents

# Introduction

There are many books about mental models on the market, so thank you for choosing this one to guide the beginning of your journey. Every effort was made to ensure that each mental model was researched and discussed in depth so you can use them to reach your goals and realize your true potential. Please enjoy!

You are probably already successful. In one way or another, everyone is. You're a great mom or dad, life coach, or football coach. You excel in the classroom or at your part-time weekend job. You own the floor of the conference room, or you own the floor of the salon. At some point during the week, you are the champion of something.

But as certain as that's a truth, so is this: there is something else to be gained from your life. There is an area of your day-to-day schedule that you wish were better. There is something that you do not excel at that you wish you did. You feel stuck. Stopped. At a dead end. You've been running ruts in the same old places, championing the same old things. It's time for a change, and you know it. That's why you're here.

This book will focus on the root of every success and every failure you've ever had. It will teach you to think about how you think and convince you that your new success story starts in a very familiar place: your own mind.

You've heard it before that thoughts become actions, actions become habits, and habits become your destiny (cite source). Now is the time to put that to the test. Introducing: mental models.

Mental models are the set of lenses you see the world through. They're the principles you use to guide your life. You use mental models when making important decisions, like whether to take that job across the country or stay closer to home and family. You use mental models at work when your boss is micromanaging your projects. You use mental models when you're making a to-do list.

Picture this: you're in line at a cafe with a few friends grabbing lunch. The line behind you is hectic: a toddler is screaming, and her mother is talking over her to soothe the nervous breakdown that's about to occur. A man in a suit a few people back is on his phone, furrowing his eyebrows and practically shouting over the mother and her child. People are elbowing each other to get closer to the menu on the wall. You're staring down the menu yourself, decoding the tiny lettering on the chalkboard into choices, when all of a sudden, you hear your name being called. Your friends have ordered, and now it's your turn.

The line swells behind you, and you blurt out, "I'll have whatever they're having," just to get out of the way. Sound familiar? Then you've used a mental model called social proof. It's a theory that says when you're unsure about something, even as small as a sandwich, and especially if you're under added pressure, as the roaring crowd of a cafe line behind you, you might just do what everybody else is doing.

How about this one: activation energy. It's a term probably faintly ringing a bell in the back of your brain because you learned about it in high school Chemistry or Physics in college. In science, this term denotes the energy from a chemical with a potential reactant needed to create the desired chemical reaction. In everyday life, however, this term is a mental model meaning the minimal amount of energy necessary to get something done.

Last week when you sent three loads of laundry through the washer and dryer and then set them in their baskets at the foot of your bed to be folded later? You were exercising this mental model: activation energy.

Even your seven-year-old nephew uses mental models. When he tugs at your pant leg or follows you around the kitchen island asking, "Why? Why? Why," until he's satisfied, he's using the mental model Proximate Versus Root Cause. If he asked you why you're hiding in the kitchen instead of hanging out in the living room with the rest of the family, and you gave him a "distal cause," (an answer that's correct but isn't the exact reason why), he will continue to ask until the "root cause" (the exact heart of the issue) is found.

So why does it matter? If you're already using mental models unknowingly, how can harnessing them help you find your purpose, enhance your happiness, and strengthen your relationships? The way you think determines the way you act, and the way you act determines where you're going. If you want to have a better relationship with your parents, it starts in your mind, with your thoughts: you have to rethink the relationship you already have with them. Maybe you blame them for things that happened in the past, and you have to work on forgiving them first. Maybe you think that as parents, it's their responsibility to reach out to you first to mend the relationship. If you continue to think in this pattern, the same way you always have, your relationship will never change. But if you really want to have a better relationship with your mom and dad, you will reframe it in your mind. You will change your thoughts, which will change your actions.

Mental models are a tool to change those thoughts. If you struggle with self-image, you can't just say, "I'm going to be more confident now," and wake up one day feeling like a rock star. You need tools to get you there. You need new ways of thinking that don't come from yourself.

This book will introduce several new mental models that you can put into place. Even if you're just now learning about mental models for the first time, these will help you to achieve your goals because you're thinking about them in a new way you never have before.

The key to using mental models successfully is using them purposefully, and that's exactly what the following chapters will discuss. Success in any form starts in your mind. It starts with an idea, a passion, or motivation.

The difference between people who get what they want and people who don't is what those people choose to do after the lightning strikes them. The next chapter will outline three people who had a goal, just like you and chose to get serious about using mental models to propel their passions forward.

One man is known for his brilliance. He's turning the world as we know it upside down, and he's wildly successful. Why? Because he thinks differently than any other entrepreneur out there. He has big plans for outer space, for smartphone technology, and automobiles. Oh, and he's a billionaire.

The next mental model creator we'll learn about is a scientist whose discoveries have prevailed since the 1930s, and are still applicable to your life, your thoughts, and your dreams today.

Finally, we'll discover a huge name in mental models, and how he used a plethora of them to gain his wealth as an investor and a businessman.

Think of the first time you realized you felt stuck and the chain of events that led you to that moment. Think of the things that crossed your mind as you read the description for this book and decided it was time to change your mind to change your life. Take a moment right now before you go on to the next chapter and decide what this book is going to do for you. Hone in on your goals until they're crystal-clear in your mind. Are you ready to achieve them?

# Chapter 1: A History of Popular Mental Models

## Elon Musk and the First Principles Mental Model

If you've been on the internet at any point in the past couple of decades, you know who Elon Musk is. He's the CEO of Tesla, a car manufacturer geared toward mass-producing affordable electric cars, solar roofs, and battery products. He's the man behind PayPal, which started as X.com and was later acquired by eBay (making Musk his first billion dollars).

As a ten-year-old, he taught himself to program computers, and as a twelve-year-old, he sold his first creation (a videogame called Blastar). He is currently involved with a few ground-breaking projects, such as Nueralink, which is a tiny implant in the brain that connects through Bluetooth to a smartphone. Simply said, Elon Musk might be one of the most brilliant and successful men today, and he uses mental models.

One, in particular, Musk is known for citing in interviews is called the first principles model. This model reaches all the way back to the Classical period (and to the Greek philosopher that probably ruled your Psychology and English classrooms: Aristotle). Aristotle believed that every instance of new philosophical belief began by tracing the belief backward until the thinker reached the original, baseline truths the belief was built upon. Rene Descartes thought similarly that philosophy could be fleshed out by doubting everything about the belief until he came to the simple truth buried beneath the philosophy (one that could no longer be doubted because it was absolutely true). Using the first principles model, these famous philosophers worked to create original thoughts instead of looking at other thoughts and changing them incrementally to make a new version of the same thought. In simpler terms, this mental model seeks to break down complicated problems to turn them into original solutions.

The principle works by taking the complicated problem and, like Aristotle and Descartes, reducing it into simple truths until it's boiled down so far that it absolutely cannot be deduced any further. With the first principles method, you won't reason from analogy or what you've seen done, but rather from the bones of the problem itself. Instead of asking, "How have I seen this done before and how can I modify that to work for me," ask yourself, "What am I absolutely sure is true in this instance, and how can I build from there?".

In 2002, Elon Musk decided to send a rocket to Mars: something that had never been done before. He set off on a mission to make it happen and quickly ran into a huge roadblock: rockets are expensive. Even after shopping around the world at different aerospace manufacturers, he found that a rocket would cost somewhere around $65 million. Famously, using the first-principles mental model, Musk began to boil down the problem (rockets are expensive) by asking, "What are rockets made of?" After compiling an ingredients list, he researched each product for their cost as a stand-alone item.

It turned out that buying the pieces for a rocket was only about two percent of the cost of buying a ready-made rocket. In this case, using the first-principles model led to Musk building a rocket himself by purchasing each product separately and launching a world-changing company to do it: SpaceX.

Space Exploration Technologies Corporation was born in 2002 and is Musk's third company. Since the establishment, SpaceX has accomplished incredible things and made history on several accounts. In 2008, NASA awarded the company with a contract to carry supplies to the International Space Station for astronauts stationed there instead of using their own shuttles. Elon Musk is brilliant, but these insurmountable achievements are partly, if not totally, because he refused to go along with the status quo and instead used a mental model to think in a different way.

That's a great story, but we're not all out here building rockets to send to outer space. Not all of us are engineers, or science-driven, or billionaires. But we all have complicated problems that can be simplified into original solutions. One of those complicated problems we all deal with at some point during our lives is the dreaded P-word: purpose.

It's one of those huge life questions that it seems a person has to answer at some point to feel totally fulfilled. "What is my purpose? Why am I here? How am I going to make a difference?" Like anything else, there is a typical track to "finding your purpose."

It usually begins at high school graduation. As late teenagers, we attempt to boil down our interests and skills into a single or a couple of words that will fit into a college major. We go to school, we graduate, we get a job, we make a family, and we call it a day. If you dropped out of college, or your path didn't work out as cleanly as that short sentence did, you may be struggling to find the answer to this question. In typical human form, you may be looking around at what other people do. You scan over lists of career aptitudes until you find one that makes you think, "Hey, I could do that!" Then you boil it down to a college major, go to school, graduate, rinse, wash, and repeat.

This is the normal path to the greater question: "What is my purpose?" This is the path of buying a rocket outright even though it's incredibly expensive. So, what is the alternative here?

You can use the same first-principles model that gained Elon Musk success and fame. All you have to do is simplify what you want to do with your life into the smallest, most deducible truths. Suppose someone told you early on that you should be a special needs teacher because you have a unique compassion for people living with disabilities. The first-principles mental model asks you, "What do you know to be true?" In this case, what you know to be true is you feel comfortable around people with disabilities and feel special compassion for them.

That's your truth, and you can do any number of things with it without having to fit the model everyone else follows. You can create products that ease the way of life for people confined to wheelchairs. You can lead online or in-person classes designed to teach able-bodied people how to treat others with special needs respectfully.

Once you have boiled down the things that excite you and motivate you to their simplest forms, you can dream as big as you want. You don't have to simply take someone else's path and tailor it to your life. You can pave your own path and make your own life from scratch and come out successfully, just like Elon Musk did with SpaceX. That's the first-principles model.

## Ivan Pavlov and Classical Conditioning

If you have any interest in Psychology or were forced to take a general education requirement at some point, the name Ivan Pavlov might ring a bell. Pavlov was a Russian physiologist that made a serendipitous discovery that changed the world of mental models and psychology forever. His experiment wasn't on people, though: Pavlov was studying canines when this epiphany struck.

The year was 1890, and Pavlov's lab room was overtaken by dogs and dog food. His theory was that when a dish of food is placed in front of a dog, it will stimulate a response: salivating. He would have his assistant place a dish of food in front of the dog and then measure the amount of salivation produced in the dog's cheek. After time went by, though, Pavlov realized something was occurring that he didn't expect.

He noticed that the dogs actually began to salivate before they even saw the food in front of them. They were triggered to begin salivating as soon as they heard Pavlov's assistant walking down the hall to bring the food into the room. The dogs had somehow learned that the approaching footsteps of Pavlov's assistant were related to their dinnertime, which triggered the response: salivating.

Fascinated, Pavlov began another series of experiments. He played the metronome (similar to the rhythm of his assistant's tapping feet) for the dogs. Not surprisingly, hearing the metronome by itself didn't make the dogs salivate. Then he began the learning process, which he calls conditioning. He played the metronome just before the dogs were fed.

After repeating this procedure over and over again, he played the metronome on its' own, without giving the dogs any food. At this point, however, the dogs had learned that the sound of the metronome was supposedly linked with eating time. Even without being presented with food, this time upon hearing the metronome's tones, the dogs began to salivate just as if their food were right in front of them.

Thirty years later, a psychologist named John Watson reads about Pavlov's discoveries, and thinks to himself, "Could classical conditioning work for humans, too?" He decided to conduct a horrifying set of experiments on an infant called Little Albert using the same experimental process Pavlov had used with his dogs. Watson showed the nine-month-old several objects on their own to note his responses to them (much like Pavlov sounding the metronome at the beginning of the experiment).

Little Albert was surprisingly unemotional when approached with a rabbit, a white rat, and even a few scary masks. What Watson did find, though, was that making a loud noise behind Little Alberts's head frightened him so much he would burst into tears immediately (in this case, Albert crying out of fear is related to the dogs salivating out of hunger). Watson then began to condition the poor baby.

He would show Little Albert the white rat, and soon after, would make the loud noise just behind Little Albert to scare him (the equivalent of Pavlov sounding the metronome and then displaying the food dish). After seven trials over seven weeks, Little Albert only had to see the white rat before he would burst into tears, without the frightening noise ever occurring.

He had learned that the rat was associated with a loud, scary noise. Just like the dogs had learned by association that the metronome meant food was approaching, Albert learned that the rat meant a scary noise was coming.

That was just the beginning. Classical conditioning is much more than just salivating dogs or scaring babies. In fact, whether you notice it or not, classical conditioning is probably already a part of your world. Remember that time you got food poisoning the day after a cookout, and now refuse to eat hot dogs? How about the night you drank too much tequila and looking at the bottle the next day made you queasy? Each of these is an example of classical conditioning. Your body has associated hot dogs, or tequila, with throwing up.

Granted, if the association only occurred once, rather than several trials over time, the association will be weaker. You might be eating hot dogs or drinking tequila again in no time. But imagine if you put this mental model into practice on purpose to achieve goals that aren't necessarily fun to do on their own.

For example, say every time you sit down and organize your budget, you reward yourself with a latte or a candy bar. After several trials over several weeks, just thinking of your electricity bill or your car payment might make you smile, thinking of foamed milk or melt-in-your-mouth chocolate. If you associate something mundane, like doing your budget, with something pleasurable, like a latte, you might even look forward to checking up on how your money is doing. Conditioning yourself this way means you will find a way to work unpleasant habits that really need to be done into your schedule more often. Let's walk through the phases of classical conditioning and see how it's done.

First, there are some important terms for you to know as you begin your own classical conditioning experiment.

- An unconditioned stimulus creates an unconditioned response.

- A neutral stimulus creates no response.

- The pairing of the unconditioned stimulus and the neutral stimulus elicits a conditioned response because the unconditioned stimulus is present.

It sounds a lot more complicated than it is. You can do this, I promise. Just hang in there! The first two linked terms are the 'unconditioned stimulus,' which produces an 'unconditioned response.' In Pavlov's experiment, the unconditioned stimulus was the food, and the unconditioned response to that stimulus was salivating. For Little Albert, his unconditioned stimulus was the scary sound, and his unconditioned response to that scary sound was crying.

Simply put, an unconditioned stimulus is something that is already present in your life and produces a response from you without any learning or conditioning needed. When the unconditioned stimulus is presented to you, you have a natural response to it. If you already like chocolate (unconditioned stimulus), your response when you eat it (joy!) doesn't have to be learned. Eating chocolate (unconditioned stimulus) elicits joy (unconditioned response). For your purposes, choose an unconditioned stimulus, or reward, that really motivates you to get something done in order to enjoy it! Still with me?

The next term is "neutral stimulus." For Pavlov, it was the sounding of the metronome. For Little Albert, it was seeing the white rat all on its' own. For our example, it will be the annoying or taxing habit you really *should* do but really don't *want* to do. Maybe it *is* budgeting. Budgeting, or whatever annoying habit you want to condition yourself to like (neutral stimulus), at this moment creates no response from you.

Here's the most complicated part. If chocolate (unconditioned stimulus) elicits joy (unconditioned response), then when it is paired with budgeting (neutral stimulus) which usually creates no response, then the conglomeration of the two (unconditioned stimulus and neutral stimulus) will illicit the now-conditioned stimulus, joy. See what's happening here? You're training your mind to think that budgeting is as pleasurable as chocolate is. Let's go over that one more time:

- An unconditioned stimulus creates an unconditioned response.

  o Chocolate elicits joy.

- A neutral stimulus creates no response.

- o Budgeting elicits no response.

- The pairing of the unconditioned stimulus and the neutral stimulus elicits a conditioned response because the unconditioned stimulus is present.

  - o Eating chocolate while you budget elicits joy because chocolate is present.

Now you try. What is an unpleasurable habit or task item that you really should do more often? What is a motivational, driving force you can reward yourself with to get that done? Maybe you'd like to drink less soda and replace it by drinking more water. You could keep a soda and a water bottle with you during the day, and every time you finish a water bottle, you get to drink a soda.

Maybe you have a hard time getting out of bed in the morning, and it makes you late to work (who hasn't been there?). You could buy a special kind of coffee (or coffee creamer) and reward yourself with it in the morning you get out of bed without pressing snooze the second time.

Whatever your habit might be, classical conditioning is a mental model that can definitely help.

Tips for Using Pavlov's Classical Conditioning:

- Don't get too hung up on the lingo. Choose a habit you don't like to do but wish you did more often and pair it with something you do like. It's as simple as that.
- The trick to using this mental model is repetition over time. Remember: Little Albert wasn't afraid of the white rat when the experiments began. It was seven weeks later, after seven separate trails, that the conditioning really began to set in. Give yourself at least a month before you decide to quit.
- Choose an unconditioned stimulus (or reward) that is easily accessible (and preferably, doesn't require anyone else to execute). You want your unconditioned stimulus to be readily available, so you're not stuck one day budgeting without your chocolate.

## Charlie Munger, Warren Buffet, and Cognitive Biases

Dairy Queen and Pampered Chef: if you haven't heard of these next giants in mental models history, then you've definitely heard of these two companies their business owns. Berkshire Hathaway is the fourth-largest public company in the world, and its' CEO and Vice Chairman use a model of over one hundred mental models to make their financial decisions.

Warren Buffet and Charlie Munger are men from Omaha, Nebraska. They met through a mutual friend at a dinner party there, where they realized they had both worked at the same local grocery store as teenagers. The rest is history. The duo has been friends for over sixty years, and business partners for over four decades.

Warren Buffet has had a knack for finances since his youth, buying his first stock at eleven years old and cultivating several businesses as a teenager, including a profitable pinball machine business in local barbershops.

He graduated from Columbia University and began work at a law firm in New York with his mentor.

After the firm closed, Buffet returned home to create his own business, Buffet Partnerships, in 1956. This business quickly accrued wealth after expanding into seven different partnerships, and as a 32-year-old, Buffet enjoyed life as a millionaire. Eventually, Buffet merged the partnerships (first as a textiles company and then moving to insurance), and Berkshire Hathaway was born.

Meanwhile, Charlie Munger attended Harvard Law School and co-founded a law firm, Munger, Tolles, & Olson, LLP (which still exists today). Buffet eventually convinced Munger to leave the practice to harness his full potential as the Vice Chairman of Berkshire Hathaway in 1978. These two friends, with a combined net worth of over $80 billion, continue to work with no announcement of retirement in the future, even at 95 and 88 years old.

Their incredible wealth and success are, you guessed it, due partially to their adherence to mental models. What's interesting and different about this partnership compared to the two models we've explored so far, is that Munger and Buffet don't choose just one mental model to guide their decisions: they choose a cornucopia.

The two first cited their success as mental model subscribers in Charlie Munger's Commencement speech at the Marshall Business School of University of Southern California Business in 1994. In this thirty-seven-minute speech alone, Munger alluded to at least six different mental models. He adheres to these mental models to make him a better investor, a more self-disciplined person, and a well-informed decision-maker.

Munger says that mental models are only useful if they're part of a toolkit. You have to create your own expansion of mental models to work into your everyday through the process, interacting together, for them to have the highest success rate. Rather than listing the hundreds of mental models Munger and Buffet subscribe to, let's take a look at one important factor of mental models that Munger says is the epitome of his work.

Munger asserts time and time again that limiting your potential failures is more important than appearing to be brilliant. Brilliance either fades and is forgotten about or crashes and burns because it's a prideful facade that can't be maintained. Being smart and recognizing your cognitive biases, however, limits your potential downsides.

What's a cognitive bias? It's any kind of idea that we as humans are prone to that deviate from logic or distract from mental models themselves. An important aspect of mental models Munger recognizes is their relationship with cognitive biases. Cognitive biases are really important to understand, and also very important to recognize in your own thought processes and behaviors. What kinds of biases can you be prone to? Let's do a quick crash course on a couple of popular cognitive biases.

## Cognitive Bias #1: Anchoring

Anchoring is a cognitive bias that occurs when focusing too much on a single piece of information. You hear one fact and put your blinders on, rendering yourself ignorant to the rest of the picture at hand. Disallowing as much information as possible from entering your problem-solving is a disservice to yourself.

However, if you're aware that you are typically subject to this cognitive bias, you are more likely to recognize when you're putting it into place. It's easily fixable to expand your horizon to allow more information in. Often times, this will also make it easier for you to solve the problem because you can see the entire picture.

Few things are more frazzling than popping a tire and ending up on the side of the road, especially if you lack the necessary tools to change the tire, or even the spare tire itself. In this situation, you could feel yourself slipping into despair, concentrating on how you, stranded by yourself, are going to get this tire fixed.

However, if you just read this chapter and remember thinking about the anchoring cognitive bias, you might allow yourself to sit back on your heels and take a breath. You might realize that this situation requires a little bit more creativity and information than you're currently allowing through your blinders.

Before learning about anchoring, you might have walked up the street three miles in your business casual attire and muscled a spare tire all the way back to your car to wrangle it on your own. But now, you hear Munger tsking in your head, telling you that your pride and your thirst for brilliance is allowing more room for failure. Now you are enabled to recognize your cognitive bias and usher in creativity.

Instead, you could take in more information: maybe after inspecting the tire further, you realize it's just a nail. Looking across the street, you realize further that there is a gas station where you could put more air in your tire to get it to the tire shop up the street. Once you're at the tire shop, the mechanics can replace (or maybe even patch) your tire. Another option would be to call a friend or a family member and have them (and all their unique mental models) come to help you out so you can figure it out together. There are so many more solutions when all the information is allowed to come into play.

## Cognitive Bias #2: Confirmation Bias

Another cognitive bias that may get in the way of your mental model work is the confirmation bias. This bias is in use when you have a preconceived idea about something, and you walk into the situation to gather the information that will confirm the idea you created before you ever came into contact with the situation.

In other words, you decide what you want to see, and then you see what you want to see. Confirmation bias comes into play all the time in day-to-day life, but the first example that comes to mind is a relational one.

Think about the cliché "bringing a guy home to meet your parents for the first time" story. Dad is already convinced the guy's a punk. When your boyfriend comes to the door, Dad, who has it in mind that this kid is bad news, no matter what, takes one look at his untucked shirt and spiked-up hair and thinks to himself, "This guy doesn't even care enough to make himself presentable."

Later in the night, the boyfriend shares that he works at the ice cream parlor after dropping out of college, and Dad thinks again, "No good. He's got no future." The night goes on, and more and more, Dad neglects to see all of the good aspects of the future courtship and sees only what he had decided to see before the boyfriend ever approached the door.

Boyfriend anecdote aside, confirmation bias occurs every day. We make assumptions about people based on the color of their skin, the behavior of their children, or the way they dress, and we look for clues to confirm that our narrow-minded stereotypes are correct. You expect the homeless man on the corner to be strung-out, so when he speaks to you with a slur because he's dehydrated and barely lucid, you see intoxication.

You assume that the guy who's always at the office leaves the parenting to his wife, so when he misses yet another recital, you assume it's because he doesn't care about his kids. There is always more to the picture than we expect, and operating on the assumption that your first idea is correct and then searching for information to back it up is always going to leave you flailing.

Recognizing confirmation bias will do more for you than making you a less judgmental person. It will make you a better communicator. Even you think you know what your colleague or friend or child is about to say, you might pause and allow them to speak, and be surprised by the ideas that come out. Instead of assuming what a person means by their statement, you might ask more questions and allow them to flesh out their idea, which will earn you respect points and a greater understanding of what they were trying to say.

Recognizing confirmation bias will also inform your decisions at work better. Casting aside assumptions about what a project will look like, or what kind of information you need to complete a presentation will allow you a greater vantage point to receive information that might be ground-breaking. Throwing confirmation bias to the wolves could lead to great success, just like Warren Buffet and Charlie Munger.

Tips for Recognizing Your Cognitive Biases:

- Do your own research. There are hundreds of different cognitive biases other than the ones listed here. They will all inhibit your learning, decision-making, relationships, work, and journey with mental models.

- Once you are familiar with several different kinds of cognitive biases, start to recognize them in your day-to-day interactions, and watch for patterns. Where would you have room to grow if you let go of these biases?

- Realize that this, just like anything else, is going to be a process. Conquering your cognitive biases takes time and is a massive undertaking. Be patient with your growth process.

Are you ready to learn more about these tools that names like Elon Musk, Ivan Pavlov, and Charlie Munger made their fame and their fortune with? These men may all be billionaires or millionaires and huge names in their industries, but don't let that discourage you into thinking that you can't achieve great success, too. Remember that achievements all begin in your mind. Accomplishing your goals and becoming who you were made, to begin with how you think and the way you think.

These big names all started out the same way you and I did. Elon Musk's parents divorced when he was ten. Ivan Pavlov didn't even start in the same school of thought he ended with: he actually began his studies in theology. Charlie Munger and Warren Buffet were just law school grads who at one point worked in Buffet's grandpa's grocery store.

They are all normal people who harnessed the power of their minds and trained themselves to use tools like mental models to be more successful than they'd ever dreamed. You can be just like them. You can use your thoughts to get anywhere you want to go. It starts here. Let's talk about concentration.

# Chapter 2: Concentration and Focus Using Mental Models

Concentrate. Your mom used this word as a command as your attention drifted away from your homework, sitting at the kitchen table as a kid. Concentrate. Your teacher said it and gave you a look during a test when you were making too much noise. Concentrate. You told yourself in the late-night hours as you struggled to pound out a paper or presentation and your mind was already mush.

Concentration is a word that's been used so often and for so long in our lives that we have never studied it, and especially not to learn how it can affect every level of success.

Maybe as a kid, concentration was little more than a command from your parents when you got restless or a warning from an authority figure when you were about to get in trouble. But now, concentration is the key to really utilizing mental models and an important tool to further your journey to achieve your goals.

This single word means the ability to let go of everything else in a moment- every other thought, feeling, project, or situation- and focus all of your efforts on whatever is in front of you. As a bonus, it relates to every single area of your life that you're looking to improve. Let me show you.

## Work/Business

Concentrating on one work project at a time is practicing good time management. It means that you're focusing all of your energy and resources on one project to make a quality product. When you concentrate on one thing at a time rather than doing a couple or several different projects at a time, fewer details will go overlooked.

Fewer things will fall through the cracks. You will enjoy the pride you feel when you reach the end of the project, knowing that you completed it to the best of your ability because you were able to concentrate on just that.

This is true regardless of what kind of business you're in. If you're a car salesman and you concentrate all of your energy on one family or buyer at a time, your sale will go much more smoothly because the car buyer will feel at ease with you and trust you.

If you're a full-time stay-at-home parent, concentrating on one task at a time at home will ensure that if only one task is done that day besides keeping your kid alive, it will be done well. If you're an entrepreneur, concentrating on making one idea or one product come to life will make that one product shine because you devoted all of your energy to it.

# Relationships

Concentration is also a priceless tool in relationships, especially in the realm of communication. This area of your life as it relates to concentration also has to do with time management. If you balance your time between work, relationships, and alone time well enough that you can afford to devote singular attention to each category during their allotted time period, each area will succeed much better than if the lines bled and you were forced to multi-task between them.

Your friends and family can tell when you are distracted, or your mind isn't totally concentrated on the conversation at hand. When your mind is forced to share its' concentration between two categories at once, neither area ends up with quality time. That project at work you're trying to reason out at the dinner table isn't going to be your best work anyway, because you're not devoting adequate attention to it.

At the same time, you are missing sharing in human interactions with your family, and later, you might not have any memory at all of the conversation that was had. You will have missed out on time with your loved ones while not really accomplishing anything important. It's a losing game trying to divide your attention. Concentrate on where you are.

## Finding Your Purpose

If you're on a quest to find your purpose, you will do better choosing one path and concentrating all of your energy on it than leaving several paths open and dabbling in each. The further you delve into a single path, the more you will know about it, and the more you will be able to consider whether it's really what you want to do with your life or not.

Leaving several paths open for discussion will distract you from devoting full attention to any one of them. It will take a lot longer to rule out or decide on any one path if you can't find the concentration to focus on just one. Simplify, and concentration will be easier.

Additional benefits of concentration:

- Accomplishing goals faster and more systematically

- Better-quality work or time

- Less stress and anxiety than multi-tasking

- More productive time and energy spent

- Practice helpful for time management discipline

- Improves communication and relationships

- Improves self-image and others' image of you

- Clearer mind open to more opportunities and inspiration

- A less hectic and happier life

Concentration is a self-discipline that will affect all of these realms of your life and more. This chapter will teach you about a couple of mental models that will help you grow stronger this discipline and urge you forward on the path to success.

## Scenario Analysis

Somehow, it's already Monday again. You wake up to the rude blare of your alarm sounding the signal to get up and get ready for the onslaught of the day ahead. Maybe you're headed to the morning shift at a restaurant a few miles down. Maybe you're about to go wake up the kids and get breakfast going. Maybe you're mentally preparing yourself for another nine-to-five at the office.

In any case, you push back the covers and drag yourself to the shower. You let your mind go blank as the hot water rushes over you, you dry off, and step out. You glance in the mirror as you brush your teeth and your eyes are glazed over still, not quite awake yet. At some point after your second cup of coffee, you kick into high-gear and drag out your laptop for some last-minute catch-up before the day begins, grab an apple, and jet out the door for another manic Monday.

This next mental model only requires a few minutes out of that hectic morning wake-up-and-go routine, but it will affect the rest of your day and the rest of your week. It requires a little concentration to utilize, but it will help you concentrate on what matters for the rest of the day.

It's called Scenario Analysis, and it's designed to rewire your brain from the typical action-reaction pattern to a more reasonable and focused day of decision-making. If you find yourself walking into the day totally unsuspecting and terrified of being blind-sided, this mental model is worth trying out.

The basis of this mental model is to anticipate the struggles of the day instead of going in blind. The thought is, the more you've envisioned and thought about the situations that could arise during the day, the more prepared you will be to react to them in a calm and reasonable manner when they come up.

As an additional perk, using the scenario analysis mental model will also ensure you focus on the kinds of scenarios you've imagined for the day, and when things outside of those scenarios occur, you will feel more confident tabling them for later. Rather than reacting right away to every struggle thrown at you, you will be able to organize them and deal with them one by one, because you've already thought through some of them.

This mental model seems strangely simple, but it works for all walks of life, even on a much grander scheme than the traditional day. For example, future planning like the scenario analysis mental model actually saved Royal Dutch Shell, the gas station company, from taking a hit during the oil shock of 1973.

The man responsible for the salvage is Pierre Wack, and he is the head of corporate planning for Shell. Wack already employed scenario analysis in his personal, day-to-day life, and one day, wondered what could happen if he applied it to his work. Once he did, he felt his ideas were important enough to bring to upper management.

He approached them with scenarios that could change Shell's story forever. The scary part was that all of them were completely rational scenarios that could happen any day. One such example was an accident occurring in Saudi Arabia, leading to damage in an oil pipeline, or even severance. An accident like that would cause a chain reaction that would affect Shell's profitability considerably, not to mention the skyrocketing gas prices for the consumer.

Incredibly, the higher-ups were stunned into action. They set important safeguards into place in their business, and when one of Wack's scenarios actually did occur in 1973, Shell was the only oil company in the business prepared. In two years, Shell moved from the eighth-biggest to the second-biggest oil station in the country, actually profiting in a time of disaster for other oil companies, all because they were prepared, using this mental model.

If this mental model can save a company from suffering in peril regardless of the world outside was stuck in, imagine what it could do for you day-to-day. How can taking a few minutes in the morning to envision the day ahead impact your day, your week, and your life? First off, it will improve your focus.

The temptation when you have an extra few minutes in the morning is to get a head start on juggling tasks that otherwise need to be completed throughout the day. I challenge you to fight that urge and instead spend that time envisioning the day ahead. When you spend that small amount of time concentrating on the challenges that might be coming, you'll be able to pass more confidently and smoothly through them.

Using scenario analysis before the day begins will also ensure that you're more prepared for the logistics of the day. If you know in the morning you'll only have twenty minutes for lunch; you can pack one from home instead of wasting your small lunchtime waiting in the drive-thru line. This mental model will also help you regain control of your life by enabling you to focus on one challenge at a time.

So how do you do it? Using this mental model will look different for everyone, depending on how you're best able to focus, the environment you've created, and the morning routine you're dealing with. Maybe using scenario analysis to visualize your day means locking yourself in your closet or your bathroom with your eyes closed for two minutes so your family or children can't bother you. Maybe it's the ten-minute commute in your car, where you commit to switching off the radio to talk yourself through the day. Maybe on your bus ride, you'll stick in headphones and jot down in your journal in a bullet-point list what you're expecting to happen that day.

The beautiful thing about this mental model is that it's so flexible. It can warp to meet your needs and requires very little from you. All you need to use this mental model is the concentration for as long as it takes to get through your day in your head, out loud, or on paper.

Tips for Using the Scenario Analysis Mental Model:

- Use the time you already have to complete this exercise every day. If you have to force yourself to get up early in the morning to use this mental model, you won't do it. Think about the time you "throw away" in the morning (or the night before) doing mindless tasks like scrolling through social media or zoning out to talk radio on the way to work. Instead of semi-engaging in mindless habits like these, take that time to fully engage in a system that will empower you to have a great day.

- Plan for interactions with other people as much as possible, especially if you know that certain people unnerve you and throw you off your game. If that one grumpy lady comes through the line to get a cup of coffee from you every Wednesday, think out in your head how you're going to respond to her. This mental model is like getting a first chance to run through every interaction of your day, so you get to practice before the real thing. Plan how you will respond to your boss when she knocks you down a peg in front of your coworkers. Maybe react the way you want to in your head and then re-run it to say something professional instead. If you know there's a possibility of that brain-dead colleague coming up to you to ask you yet another dumb question, figure out a way to talk to them that's not demeaning in your brain. Use this mental model as a first-take of all of your personal interactions for the day.

- Like any mental model, of course, this will take time to make a difference. If you don't feel anything different after the first day, that's okay.

In fact, it's normal. Remember that mental models are habits that take time to work.

- If you're a journal person, definitely take time to journal out your visualization of the day. A great tool to use for visualizing the day by writing is called stream of consciousness writing. To use this tool, you'll write down everything you think along the same vein as one long sentence in one stream of thought. You don't have to use punctuation or correct grammar or spelling. Just get it all out on paper. As an added practice in metacognition (thinking about your thinking), re-read through your entry after you're finished. Stream of consciousness journaling is extremely helpful for some people because standard journaling seems too daunting. Stream of consciousness writing doesn't require full sentences, punctuation, or writing a perfect sentence. It just follows the stream of your thoughts. Often, ideas or worries you didn't even know you had come out when you're not thinking about perfecting your prose.

You are all set to begin changing your days by using the scenario analysis mental model. How would your interactions change if you used this model? How would your concentration on your work benefit if you weren't worried about that annoying colleague poking his head into your office? Try it out and see what happens.

## The Circle of Competence Mental Model

Everyone you encounter on a daily basis is an expert of something. The barista who crafts your drink at the local coffee shop in the morning knows everything there is to know about how to make your caramel latte. Through a combination of experience and study, she has learned techniques to successfully steam the milk, time your espresso shot, and how to balance those ingredients with the right amount of caramel syrup. The mom swaddling her baby in line behind you at this point, probably knows everything there is to know about her child at this stage.

She knows what screams mean he's hungry and what screams mean his diaper is wet, and how to tell when he's ready for a nap. The parking officer you pass by in her fluorescent yellow vest on the way out the door is an expert of this block and the next. She knows just from a glance which meters are overdue and which will be soon. The secretary at your office is a pro at managing his boss's schedule. He could navigate tough phone calls in his sleep.

All of that being said, the person whose reflection you see glinting back at you in the bus or car window is also a master of something or several things. Maybe you're a phenomenal brother, and you know by the first 'hello' when your sibling picks up the phone what kind of day they're having. Maybe you're a master investor, as the inventors of this next mental model, and choosing which stocks to invest in is always obvious to you.

Whatever it is, you have what is called 'areas of competence,' and the Circle of Competence mental model says they are your best chance at success.

We learned about Charlie Munger and Warren Buffet in chapter one when we discussed cognitive biases that hold us back from realizing true potential. Munger and Buffet are the Vice Chairman and CEO, respectively, of the successful company Berkshire Hathaway. Now we will learn about one of the mental models these gentlemen utilize to make their company so successful.

The circle of competence mental model says that like you, each of us has areas of competence, which also means that each of us has areas of incompetence. The key to success, according to this model, is honing the skills and knowledge you already have while avoiding the areas you are not a master of. This may sound rigid, and frankly, against your mother's insistence that "you can be anything you want to be!", but hear me out.

The mental model doesn't say you can't be the master of something new. It just says that if your ultimate goal is to achieve success, you should first focus on your superpower-the unique skillset and knowledge you already have- and then slowly, over time and with discipline, expand those skillsets to include mastery of something new.

So how exactly do Charlie Munger and Warren Buffet utilize this mental model in their business? I'm glad you asked! These wealthy and successful investors use the circle of competence mental model when training their specialized investors which stocks to choose. It shows up in countless interviews and even Buffet's 1996 Shareholder Agreement, where Buffet is telling his specialized investors to invest only in what they know about.

In one of these interviews, Buffet discusses this mental model in relation to one of his top business managers. He calls her Mrs. B. Mrs. B is a Russian immigrant, and she speaks very little English. I know what you're thinking: how can you be a business manager in America, where the primary language is English, and your primary job is to do business with people verbally if you don't speak English? The English language was not one of Mrs. B's circles of competence. But the furniture was.

Mrs. B knows all about furniture. How it's made, what it's made of, what it's worth; you name it, and she knows it. That's why, despite her inability to speak English fluently, Mrs. B is the manager of the largest furniture store in Nebraska. Instead of allowing her areas of incompetence to handicap her, Mrs. B was determined and single-mindedly focused on an area of competence she knew would carry her to success. Because of this concentration, she was successful.

Throughout your life, you've built skills and knowledge through your experiences and education, just like Mrs. B. Your specialized experience and knowledge is your superpower. It's what's going to make you successful. This is also a case of quality over quantity: if you know a little about a lot of different things, you're going to be a little successful in a lot of different areas.

But if you know a lot about one thing or two things, suddenly you've got a specialization. You've got something that the guy down the block (or your barista, or your meter maid, or your secretary) doesn't have. This model asserts that it's not about being the master of every circle of competency. It's really just knowing the boundaries of your own circle of competence.

On numerous occasions, Buffet and Munger refer to themselves as "learning machines," and this mental model reflects that thinking. There's something about knowing how much more there is to learn about that propels you into that area of the unknown and motivates you to learn.

Using this mental model will encourage you to continue learning while you're honing your craft. While the most fail-safe path is to stick with what you know, you won't be able to resist the temptation of learning about what you don't and expanding your areas of competence once you've defined them.

This mental model is also an incredible exercise in recognizing what you are good at and what you do know so you can concentrate on those areas. Maybe you're sitting here thinking that you have no idea what you're an expert in because all these years, you've pushed it aside to work a job for a paycheck or to be a parent. For you, this mental model could be ground-breaking simply because it asks you to sit down and figure out what you've got that nobody else does.

So many people walk through their day-to-day, having no idea what makes them valuable. This is your opportunity to decide. Once you have a list of those skills, you will be enabled to concentrate on them and really hone in on how to improve them. You'll spend more time in your areas of competency because now you're aware of them and you know what they are.

Not only will this mental model make you a better learner, but by improving your self-awareness, it will help to improve your self-image. Firstly, using the circle of competence mental model will make you more patient with your learning curve. Instead of thinking, "I should know this," you'll think, "This is outside of my area of competence, and I am learning here." You'll also get a new-found sense of confidence, realizing how you shine in your areas of competency. You'll start to recognize the things you're undeniably a master of and that when you concentrate your energy on those things, success follows you.

Luckily, this is a mental model that you can put into place in your life right now to start realizing your areas of competency. The first step is sitting down and being totally honest with yourself about your strengths and weaknesses.

If you're a person, who likes to see things on paper, grab a sheet of paper and draw a large circle. Then draw a smaller circle inside of that first circle. Your smaller circle will represent your areas of competence, and the larger circle will represent the areas where you're not yet a master. Ask yourself questions like:

- What do I know everything about, no questions asked?

- What skill makes me feel really confident when I use it?

- What do I do well?

- What could I teach someone else to do?

- What skills and knowledge have I earned in the past?

- What skills and knowledge do I use daily, either at work, in my personal life, or enjoying my hobbies?

Use these guidelines to determine what falls into your category of competence. Don't get discouraged if it's a short list! Remember the point is not to know everything about lots of things but to know everything about just a couple of things. Also, don't miss the 'smaller' areas of mastery, concentrating on 'larger' areas.

You could have a degree in health science, deeming you a master of the inner workings of a human body, but you could also have strong communication skills. Consider both equal skillsets.

Likewise, knowing the ins and outs of your child's favorite television show could also prove to be an important circle of competency. Every bit of knowledge you've gleaned to make you a master of an area serves a purpose. All of those purposes serve you and your future success.

After you're looking at a full (or semi-full, or sort-of-full) inner circle of competent areas, think about how each of them relates in some way to your life. Question how you use each skill or pool of knowledge in the roles you play throughout the day.

Your mastery of empathy could serve in your friendships but also in the parts of your job that require customer service. Your passion for writing and editing could help when your friend's resume is in peril, but it could also serve if you decided to write a book.

Which brings us to our next point: determining how concentrating on your skillsets will aid you in your future roles and help you accomplish your goals. If you're still not even sure what your future goals are, the circle of competency is a great place to start thinking about it.

Looking at the areas you're a master of, now dream about what your future could look like if you concentrated your energy more on growing those skills or training that knowledge base. Again, if you're a naturally empathetic person, could you have a future in counseling or social work? If you bake an incredible pie, could you open a bakery or write a cookbook?

After you've done some work on your areas of competency and linked them to your future goals, take a look at the parts of those goals that don't lie within your areas of competency. What can you do to slowly build your skills to match those areas? Make opportunities for yourself to practice, learn, and grow.

Tips for Using the Circle of Competency Mental Model:

- Be completely honest with yourself about your skills and aptitudes. Set aside your pride and realize where your skills lie, and where they don't. Remember everyone has both areas, and most of the time, the areas of incompetence are bigger.

- Again, journal about it! Sometimes just thinking about an idea won't cut it. To delve into it further, write about your areas of competency and incompetency and how they relate to your life and your future success.

# Additional Tips for Concentration

The two mental models this chapter touches on give you an understanding of two ways to concentrate on bringing you success. If you're having trouble with concentration in general, here are some additional tips and tricks.

## *Set a Timer*

Even for people who excel at concentration, focusing on one project for a long period of time without knowing when the next break will be is difficult. The Pomodoro Technique is a system that will help you be productive and improve focus in easy, manageable chunks of time. It was developed by Francesco Cirillo, who at the time was a college student looking to improve his productivity levels.

Here's how it works: first, you choose a task. It could be the mountain of laundry or dishes piling up, a project for work, or a paper for school. Then, you'll set a timer for twenty-five minutes. For the next twenty-five minutes, you'll devote unconditional attention to the task you chose. After the timer rings, you'll allow yourself a short break to relax and do something unrelated to the task you chose. Go for a walk, grab a snack, zone out for a few minutes.

Then you'll reset the timer and start back up on your project again, just like the first time. After every four "pomodoros" (twenty-five-minute productive spurts), you'll allow yourself a longer break, like twenty or thirty minutes, to recharge. How many total "pomodoros" you do is up to you. And that's how it's done!

Why should you use the Pomodoro Technique instead of just blowing through tasks and projects until they're done? Although the idea of crushing a major project in one sitting is tantalizing, the truth is, it's hardly attainable. Often, these attempts end in major burn-out, frustration, and a plummeting inner monologue.

Utilizing the Pomodoro Technique forces you to set goals. You have to get to the end of the twenty-five-minute timer before you can get up and stretch or get another cup of coffee. This also means that at any given moment, there is an end in sight. When your brain starts to melt, a single glance at the timer can give you a rejuvenating sense of calm and motivation: only three minutes left to go turns into only two minutes, and then only one. When you try to simply plow through a task, there's no end in sight. No hope for the next break.

The Pomodoro Technique is also a self-discipline tool. Often, when we set forth to accomplish a task, there is either a lack of discipline or too much of it. One group of people will find themselves knee-deep in a bag of Cheetos, and a Netflix documentary they swore was just going to be on in the background.

The other camp will sit down at the desk at two in the afternoon and not allow themselves to rise from it until the task is done, even if that means staying upright until early into the morning hours. Neither is healthy, and neither is a reflection of good self-discipline. Disciplining yourself doesn't just mean getting the task done; it means balancing the importance of getting the task done with the importance of everything else going on, including your own health. Gorging yourself on work can be just as bad for you as gorging yourself on Netflix and junk food. The Pomodoro Technique is a system that keeps you motivated to balance the two needs. You can have the junk food and the completed task list. Use this technique to stay focused. Let's recap:

1. You choose a task.
2. You set a timer for 25 minutes.
3. You devote unmetered, disciplined concentration to the task you chose.
4. When the timer rings, you give yourself a short break (five or ten minutes).
5. Every four "pomodoros" (25-minute productive systems), give yourself a longer break (20 or 30 minutes).

## *Meditation*

Contrary to what your inner voice may be telling you upon reading that subtitle, meditation isn't just for hippies or yoga teachers. Millions of people meditate every morning, from successful athletes to news anchors to your checkout clerk at the grocery store.

Several successful businessmen, including the Miracle Morning author Hal Elrod, cite using meditation as a part of their routine for their wealth and success. Sure, for some people, meditation is the classic picture: sitting on a mat on the floor with legs crossed, eyes closed, and fingertips touching as they murmur 'om.' But for others, it looks like turning on a soothing voice at two in the morning to help get back to sleep. For others, it looks like using a podcast as they drive, bike, or walk to work to center their focus for the day. For still others, it looks like sitting on the bathroom floor with a cup of coffee and a journal to slow down their thoughts and get ready for what's coming.

What is meditation, then, if it's not the picture in your head? It's an amount of time you set aside during the day to be totally present in the moment and mindful of what's going on in your head, your heart, and your body. How often during a normal workday do you take a moment out and check in with what's going on inside you?

My guess is not very often. Most people say they don't have time for meditation, and very few will utilize it randomly and without a set time or place during their day. It's a discipline and one that will help you.

Allowing yourself to be completely engrossed in your thoughts and your feelings for just a few minutes of the day without any other distraction will cut down on feelings explosions that might occur at inappropriate times later. If you struggle with naming your emotions or even figuring out what's causing them, meditation is also a great resource to use to figure out what you feel and why you feel it.

It might be the only time during the day that you check in with how you are really doing, and concentrating on that aspect of yourself is essential to your success. You can be incredibly intelligent and savvy with your areas of competence, but if you make emotional decisions because you haven't harnessed how you feel or what you think, your future will be in peril.

Many users of meditation also report that consistent practice results in better focus during the day, even after their session, and catch their mind wandering less.

It improves mental toughness, which we'll read about in a later chapter, and mental toughness is often the difference between giving up and persevering. While we're talking about feelings, it's important to note that studies have shown consistent meditation in as little as three weeks heightens compassion.

A heightened sense of compassion will aid your relationship with yourself but also with your friends, family, colleagues, and boss. Compassion is an unprecedented tool for success.

Alongside the aspects of your mental health that meditation rewards are the physical rewards that being mindful can reap. Meditation improves your nights of sleep, reduces blood pressure, and helps to cut down on anxiety and stress. People who meditate are more motivated to work out and perform better during their physical exertion.

If meditation is starting to sound less daunting and more like something you should try, there are a few tips to getting you started. The first is to use a meditation app.

There are many on the market, but the few listed below are ones I have used personally used myself and reviewed for you here.

Most meditation apps have a lot in common. They all will have some sort of on-boarding process where they ask about your familiarity with meditation and subsequently provide a 'course' of meditations to get you started. After you complete that course, you can explore different categories of guided meditations, like sleep, anxiety, and focus, among others (depending on the app).

If after a while, you find that the guiding voice is distracting to your practice, a lot of them will have instrumental music or 'soundscapes' that you can use to guide your own meditation. Once you have used the app frequently, your statistics will usually be recorded in a profile dashboard you can see, with varying amounts of competition laced in.

Most of them will also provide a free trial or a set number of free meditations and then will require a paid subscription. Let's launch into looking at our first meditation app: Headspace.

## *Meditation App #1: Headspace*

Headspace is one of the most popular meditation apps out there. It's simple and easy to use and has thousands of different meditations available. Like most meditation apps, it begins with a survey asking you how comfortable you are with meditation, and then provides a first meditation course. From there, it organizes meditation into categories, like stress and anxiety, meditation basics, personal growth, kids and parenting, life challenges, and meditation for students.

It also features 'sleep casts,' which are recordings of soothing sounds, like hummingbirds and other natural sounds to help get you to sleep. It has meditations of varying lengths to encourage users of all levels and features a 'stats' page to keep track of how often you've meditated and for how many days in a row.

This app is excellent for beginners. It has a section for learning more about the basics of meditation, but it generally uses the 'dive-in' approach. The first meditation in the basics course doesn't specify much at all about how to meditate; it just launches right into the guided meditation. What's also interesting about this meditation app is it generates a list of recommended courses and single meditations for you based on the meditations you've enjoyed before.

It's probably the easiest app to use on this list and doesn't require any complicated maneuvering to get to the kind of meditation you'd like to try. The Headspace app has a two-week free trial, and after that offers yearly and monthly subscriptions.

## Meditation App #2: Insight Timer

The Insight Timer is a meditation app that incorporates thousands of different meditation teachers. This means if you don't like the style or voice cadence of one teacher, it's okay because you have thousands of others to choose from. Due to the number of teachers and different ideas they all have, there are thousands of interesting and unique topics for meditation courses.

A few popular ones include 'When Relationships End: Honoring the Process,' and 'Self-Acceptance Through Authenticity.' New courses are uploaded every day and can be found in a category called 'daily.'

This app also offers courses and single meditations for true beginners, like the 'Ten Foundations of Meditation' that literally walk you through what meditation is, how to do it, and the impact you'll see in your day-to-day life. Another interesting aspect of this app is the 'talks' section, which features podcasts on a variety of topics, both meditation-related and not. Although this app provides a foundation for new users, it also provides resources for people who have been meditating for a while, one of those resources being the timer.

After you've been meditating for a long time, you might find that you don't need a guiding voice or a music track to meditate to anymore and that you actually prefer silence. You can set the timer on this app for any longevity of time you wish your meditation session to last. There is even a setting to choose a kind of bell to ring at a set interval to remind you to refocus your thoughts.

The typical resources this app also provides include sound recordings to aid in sleep, musical tracks, and a kids' meditation section. There are thousands of free meditations offered, but as a paying member, you unlock more.

## *Meditation App #3: Calm*

The Calm app is another popular meditation tool you've probably heard of. Like most apps, this one categorizes meditations into topics like personal growth, anxiety, sleep, kids, and relationships. It offers soundscapes and instrumental musical tracks that are also organized into categories, like focus, lullabies, relax, and nature melodies.

The personal dashboard provided is also a helpful tool, tracking how many mindful days, mindful minutes, and total sessions, including your longest streak, which will keep you motivated to continue. It even includes a calendar where you can log meditations you have performed outside of the app to get credit for your streak and stats.

What makes this app different is exclusivity and specialty of their teachers and even their music. Most meditation apps use prominent teachers of the yoga or mindfulness worlds but names you and I wouldn't readily recognize.

The Calm app has an entire adult bedtime story section as told by voices like the actor Matthew McConaughey, English comedian Stephen Fry, and even animal expert Bindi Irwin. The section also includes a recording of the Economics teacher from the famous movie Ferris Bueler's Day Off reading aloud the first chapter of Wealth of a Nation by Adam Smith. His monotone voice will lull you to sleep in no time.

Another exciting addition to these bedtime stories is a series called Painted Dreams with Bob Ross, in which

Bob Ross describes every step of completing a painting as you drift off to sleep. The app's music section also includes albums that are only available on Calm, like Liminal Sleep by Sigur Ros.

Overall, the voices of this app were the most unique characteristic. The Calm app provides a one-week free trial and then offers paid subscriptions after that.

## Meditation App #4: 10% Happier

Right off the bat, this app will pique your interest with an introductory video by the CEO Dan Harris, who is not a yoga guru, mental health coach, or mindfulness expert, but a news anchor. Harris' goal for this app is to demonstrate that meditation and mindfulness aren't just for one kind of person and doesn't just belong on your to-do list. He fully believes that meditation should be a practice that permeates the rest of your life. Keeping with that belief, the meditations offered are recorded by a number of masters of other fields, like neuroscience professor at Vanderbilt University, David Vago, Ph.D., and even a few by the CEO himself.

The app, like the Insight Timer app, also features a 'Talks' section: a collection of podcasts ranging in topics. A few include topics like "In Praise of Sadness," detailing how grief paves the road for joy, and "Escape from Zombieland," telling you in five minutes how mindfulness can bring you back to life.

The 10% Happier app also includes all of the typical perks: an upfront survey when you sign up, a populated beginner course to get you started, and categorized sections including sleep meditations. A distinct difference about this app that none of the others mentioned so far include, however, is the option to ask a question of a meditation coach.

One tap of the button connects you with an actual, live person with at least a decade of meditation experience to message about whatever you're having trouble within meditation.

The 10% Happier app provides a seven-day free trial and then offers options for monthly or yearly subscriptions.

Tips for Meditation:

- Longevity is more important than duration. Doing a minute-long meditation every day for three weeks will be more helpful than doing a fifteen-minute meditation once a month. Consistency is key.

- Make it part of your routine. Decide on a time and place, and a length of time you're willing to meditate.

- Use a guide, like an app above or even a recording online.

- Try to meditate first thing in the morning, or earlier in your day, so meditation doesn't get pushed to the back burner behind the rest of your to-do list.

- During meditation, breathe naturally, and sit comfortably. Don't allow the picture of meditation in your head to decide what your meditation has to look like.

- Don't shy away from being uncomfortable. It's going to be uncomfortable to be that present and recognize your thoughts and feelings all at once in a concentrated time frame.

- Use meditation to create mindful goals. Decide what you're going to take from the session to go through your day.

- After meditating, check in with yourself. Do you feel any different? Did you make any major epiphanies?

- If you have trouble sticking with it, get some accountability by doing it with a friend. Text each other when you complete your meditation session for the day to keep each other on track.

- Don't judge yourself or your session. There's no such thing as a 'bad' session. You showed up. That's what matters.

At the end of the day, no matter where you'd like to apply a more disciplined view of concentration in your life, that's the key to succeeding: showing up. Every day you have a choice to be present and be involved in your future or to simply be a walking ghost.

You can decide you don't feel like it today and go through the motions as other people do, but here's the thing:

you're not like other people. That's why you bought this book, that promised to help you build a stronger toolkit to achieve your goals.

That's why you've spent time reading it, and you've gotten this far. You aren't a person who decides that just walking through the day is okay. You're a person that wakes up in the morning thinking, "Today is an opportunity. I am going to learn something today. I am going to be better today than I was yesterday."

You are a person who concentrates on their goals. You are a person who radiates confidence and motivation. Congratulate yourself on showing up, all of you, today. Then do it tomorrow.

# Chapter 3: Mental Models and Self-Discipline

Everyone hates the word "discipline." An utterance or thought of the word alone can conjure groans and sighs. When we think of discipline, we think of withholding joy from ourselves. When we think of discipline, we imagine self-deprivation in exchange for chores we really don't want to do. But what if we didn't think of self-discipline as a punishment? What if we thought of it as just another way to achieve our goals, make it easier to get where we're going, and even make the day-to-day more enjoyable?

The truth is, putting self-disciplining habits into place will reduce stress, engage your goals and dreams, make time for things you enjoy, improve your relationships, and make you an across-the-board more successful, happier person. We think that self-discipline doesn't really relate to our day-to-day lives once we're adults, but some habits of successful individuals actually rely heavily on self-discipline.

Things like getting up on time, working out, practicing dental hygiene, and maintaining relationships (both at work and in your personal life) all require some amount of self-discipline. Self-discipline can better all areas of life, including health, friendships, and romantic relationships, mental illnesses like anxiety and depression, work and school, and more.

It may surprise you, but oftentimes, our biggest struggles are also actually directly related to our lack of self-discipline. If you're up all night the day before a huge presentation, hating yourself for not preparing during the weeks leading up to it, you lack time-management. And time management is, you guessed it, a skill that takes self-discipline to foster. If you're stuck in a rough place financially and can't seem to get out of the rut of living paycheck-to-paycheck and having an abysmally low savings account (or none at all), you might be lacking self-discipline. Life without self-discipline (or even with little self-discipline) is actually living the high road.

A life with strong self-discipline habits, however, is a prosperous one. Living with self-discipline means being able to organize days that feed all aspects of your well-being: time for work, for friends and family, and time for yourself. Living with self-discipline means living less stressfully because you trust that you've taken care of what needs to be done, rather than leaving it to your future self to clean up your messes. So how can you begin to build self-discipline into your life? With mental models, of course.

# The Eisenhower Matrix

You've heard it before: time-management is essential. But why? Having habits that assist with managing your time well means a better self-image, more success at work and school, higher respectability, and improved relationships, among other things. Being able to clear out your task list consistently leads to feelings of success and confidence.

You will enjoy getting to the end of the day and be more motivated to get going at the beginning of the day when your self-talk sounds like, "I can do this! I crushed it yesterday!". You'll be more successful professionally with time management skills, regardless of what that looks like for you. Being able to prioritize projects to meet deadlines and spend quality time on them is essential for workplace success.

Others will notice when you step up your game, too, and you'll be better liked and more respected as a colleague. Time management also means a happier spouse and happier friends. If you can balance your career, dreams, and miscellaneous tasks, you will be more focused on your loved ones and giving them quality time while you're with them.

Even with all of these perks of time-management, many people still struggle to implement the habits necessary to upkeep it. It seems too daunting to tackle, or their life is too hectic to set aside an hour to plan and prioritize. People who don't make time to plan their time, however, suffer much more than people who do. Lack of time management is often linked to higher rates of stress, anxiety, and depression.

People who don't plan their time accordingly don't sleep as well, or as much, and have a never-ending merry-go-round of tasks circling behind their eyelids when they finally do shut. They have trouble balancing their work and home lives, and their relationships suffer for it.

Time management takes discipline and doesn't happen overnight. However, it is possible for anyone willing to put in the work to gain this skill, implement these habits, and enjoy a happier, fuller life. It starts with learning how to prioritize.

There are few better examples of productive life than President Dwight D. Eisenhower. During his two terms in office as the 34th president, President Eisenhower began programs that would work to create the highway system in the United States, launch the internet, and explore outer space with NASA.

But that's not all. Before Eisenhower was President of the United States, he was also a Commanding General of the Allied Forces during World War II, a five-star general in the Army, the first Supreme Officer of NATO in 1951, and President of Columbia University. It's also said that he found time to enjoy alone time by golfing and oil painting. It's safe to say President Eisenhower had a lot on his plate (and knew how to handle it).

One of his most powerful (and easiest to use) time management tools is the Eisenhower Matrix, also known as the Eisenhower Box. This mental model is about to blow your to-do list out of the water. Introducing this principle to your self-discipline toolbox will completely rethink how you prioritize your time.

|  | Urgent | Not Urgent |
|---|---|---|
| Important | Do<br><br>Do it now. | Decide<br><br>Schedule it for later. |
| Not important | Delegate<br><br>Can someone else do it for me? | Delete<br><br>Eliminate it. |

As you can see, the Eisenhower Matrix breaks tasks down into four different boxes or categories. These boxes are organized by urgent to not-as-urgent and important to not-as- important. The first category, located in the box in the upper left-hand corner is the "Do First" category.

These are the most urgent and most important tasks in your task list, and they need to be done as soon as possible. Tasks of this nature will be things like getting a prescription refilled or completing work on a project that's due soon. Any task items that should not be put off any longer should go in this category. President Eisenhower asserts that setting a timer and doing these tasks as soon as you can is the best policy.

Moving on to the second category, or the box in the upper right-hand corner is home to the important but less-urgent tasks: the "Decide" box. These are to-do-list items that are important to be done but can wait until a little later to be completed. These tasks will be things like getting your oil changed or folding that laundry that's still sitting at the foot of your bed.

Tasks that should be done pretty soon but don't necessarily have a deadline (or have a deadline that's approaching but not soon) should go in this box. Items in the "Decide" box are tasks that need to be scheduled to do at a certain time in the future. Make sure to set the time aside and even put it in your calendar or planner to ensure these tasks don't get put off any longer than necessary.

The third category on the bottom left-hand corner is the "Delegate" box. These are tasks that are time-sensitive but not as important and can possibly be handed off to someone else to complete.

The purpose of this category is to recognize when projects don't necessarily need your attention; they just need someone's attention. For example, if you are engaged in a category one or two task and your husband calls to ask if you'll pick up some dog food on the way home, you can give him the necessary information (the kind of dog food) to complete the task himself, delegating a category three task to someone else. The important thing to note about this category is you have to keep track of who you delegated what task to so you can follow up with that person later.

The last category is for tasks that are neither important nor urgent, and these tasks belong in the "Eliminate" box. Things that go in the "Eliminate" category get in the way of your productivity and inhibit your ability to knock off tasks in the first, second, and third category. These can be unhelpful habits, like social media scrolling, or useless tasks that are taking up time and don't need to be completed at the moment, like buying new work shoes just for the sake of going shopping.

This category may require the most self-discipline because it necessitates you to say "no" to yourself when you want to do things that are not productive. This isn't to say that things you like to do in your free time that aren't work-oriented, like reading or watching TV, should go in this category.

The goal of time management is to balance your time between work and personal life so you can make room for free time to do the things you want to do. This category is simply for items on your to-do list that are just taking up space and aren't time-sensitive or important at the moment. Remember: your most important resource is time.

Tips for Using the Eisenhower Box:

- Limit how many tasks you put into each quadrant. When you get five in each quadrant, complete the most important or time-sensitive task in the "Do" category. You don't want to collect tasks. You want to finish them.

- Only use one list for all areas of your life (business, personal, housework, family, etc.), so you don't have to worry about neglecting one list or the other.

- Don't allow others to tell you what your priorities are or should be. This is your to-do list to manage your time, and you should write it with yourself in mind.

## BJ Fogg's Tiny Habits Mental Model

How many times have you thought about making a big change, or latching onto a big goal, and given up because you were afraid you couldn't? If we were in an auditorium right now, and someone on stage had asked that question, every person's hand would be in the air. It happens to everyone.

It's easy to get discouraged when something you want seems like an insurmountable, inordinately gigantic deal. It's even harder to look at a colossal goal like that and break it down into smaller pieces to know where to start. Maybe you've been trying to lose the last thirty pounds for months now, and you've just given up. Maybe you would really love to go back to school, but you're intimidated by the process of getting there. Maybe you're sick and tired of feeling inadequate, and you want to plunge into a journey of self-love, but you have no idea where you'd even start or how you'd get the resources to do so. Everyone at some point or another has been there. It just seems too big.

BJ Fogg, the Director of the Behavior Design Lab at Stanford University, was right where you are. Fogg has studied behavior science for two decades, and yet one day, found himself at a plateau in his weight loss journey. He began to experiment, using what he knew about behavior, to jolt himself out of this plateau and get back into losing the weight he'd set out to lose at the beginning of the journey. He bought an electronic scale, hoping that just stepping on it every day and seeing the number would motivate him. It didn't. He started logging his daily weight on Twitter every day to see if that would help. It didn't.

Finally, he realized that only three things really change behavior: having an epiphany, changing your environment, or taking a small step. Based on these last two principles, Fogg created the Tiny Habits Method, an easily accessible mental model for self-discipline.

Fogg's Tiny Habits Method is centered around making one tiny step toward one colossal goal one day at a time. Sounds silly, right? But it works. When adhered to, this mental model creates long-lasting, long-term results, by changing behavior in tiny increments, as the name suggests.

The first step is a little bit like the First Principles mental model we learned about through Elon Musk. First, we'll think about the outcome we want to see (for Fogg, it was losing weight). Then we'll work backward, thinking about the behaviors that lead to that outcome, paring them down bit by bit until we find one very simple behavior that can change to encourage the outcome. For weight loss, it can be increasing water consumption, limiting stress, working out, or any other number of behaviors. Then you choose one tiny behavior to turn into a habit. For Fogg, it was push-ups.

Then, Fogg asserts, you have to understand that in order for the behavior to work, you have to have the motivation to do it, the ability to do it, and finally, a trigger (or a call to action) to complete the behavior. This last part is crucial: the call to action works best if it's something that happens in your schedule every day anyway. Something you don't have to put in extra effort or go out of your way to complete. Adhering to these guidelines, Fogg decided that to accomplish his outcome of losing more weight; he would do two push-ups every time he went to the bathroom.

That's right. Every time he flushed after using the restroom during the day, he dropped to the floor and did two push-ups. It seems silly, right? Like it would never work? Just by doing push-ups every time he used the bathroom every day, Fogg lost five pounds, and then ten, and then twenty, all in the course of a few months. It really works.

So, what does that mean for you? How could engaging in this mental model and trying it out help you achieve more self-discipline? Firstly, if you create a tiny habit and persist in doing it for several weeks or months, you'll reap the results of the goal you've set. You'll lose the pounds, or write the book, or kick your caffeine addiction.

What else? Creating a tiny habit and sticking with it will also give you practice in developing and staying with new habits that are good for you. Part of self-discipline is determining habits whose end results will benefit you in the long run and then having the perseverance to continue to work on those habits. In the meantime, you will be gaining a heightened sense of self-worth and motivation to succeed. You'll start to realize that your success (or your failure) is your responsibility. It's up to you if you accomplish your goal or not. It's not luck or fate that are responsible for your success. It's your work ethic and your perseverance that carry you to the finish line.

Tips for Using the Tiny Habits Method:

- Watch BJ Fogg's talk at TedxFremont on YouTube

- Choose a result you're passionate about and motivated to succeed. You have to want it!

- Choose a behavior you're able to do.

- Choose a trigger, or call to action, for your behavior that happens every day anyway, so it's easier for you to do the behavior

- Choose a small enough behavior

- Invite a friend to share your journey or make their own tiny habit alongside you

- Celebrate! You're on your way!

Revisit the goals you set as you began reading this book. Are any of them related to a lack of self-discipline? How could you use the Eisenhower Matrix or the Tiny Habits Method to rectify them? Keeping these two mental models in mind as you go through your week will help build disciplines that will make you a happier and more successful person. However, these are only two of many mental models out there that exist to build self-discipline habits. Do some research of your own to find new mental models that could help you on this journey, too.

Remember that self-discipline can manifest itself in all corners of your life. When you drag yourself out of bed in the morning instead of pressing snooze on the alarm again, you're practicing good self-discipline. When you sit down with a friend to have a serious conversation about an argument you had the week before instead of avoiding the confrontation, you're practicing good self-discipline. Celebrate the small victories and pat yourself on the back when you recognize yourself adhering to a habit that will lead to better self-discipline. You can do this!

# Chapter 4: Mental Toughness Training

Mental toughness. Google these words, and you will find millions of hits with anecdotes about Olympic athletes, West Point graduates, and military personnel. You will also find stories of how people just like you used this high-class skill to reach new heights in their own lives.

Mental toughness is the key skill that makes the difference between a benched high school baseball pitcher going pro and never playing again. It's the difference between the Etsy shop that just kind of peters out and one that becomes the owner's full living. It's the difference between your stagnancy and your glowing future. Another, simpler word for mental toughness that you've probably heard before is this: grit.

Determination. Perseverance. More than intelligence or genes or talent, this is the stuff that's been shown to set successful people apart from the rest. It's the drive to achieve long-term goals, even when it's tough, or you don't feel like it. Even when roadblocks rise up to defeat you, with grit, you won't back down.

At the very core of mental toughness is consistency. Once you create a goal, consistently striving toward it every day, one step at a time, is what's going to earn you grit. If you're an artist or want to be, that looks like creating something, even if it's small, every single day without failing. If you're an athlete, it looks like showing up early to practice every single time, completely focused and ready to go, and never missing a workout. If you're a nurse, it looks like showing up for your patients, even when you're tired, in any form they need you to be.

The great news about mental toughness is this: you can have it. That voice in your head, that's been telling you someone else deserves your dreams because they're just more talented or have better skills than you, is wrong. Talent and genetics can be completely overrun by one person who has the drive and the willpower to focus hard on getting where they want to be. Anyone can achieve mental toughness. That anyone includes you.

Being mentally tough means, you'll be better prepared for change. It means you'll be more positive under pressure, more productive during the workday, and harness more emotional stability. It means you'll grow into the part of yourself that believes your happiness has nothing to do with your external world and everything to do with your internal world.

Being mentally tough means, you'll focus on your goals and dreams instead of just reacting to life as it comes.

You'll be more patient with the outcomes because you can see clearly how you're getting there, and you'll experience a more relaxed, content countenance. All of this can be yours. Are you ready to begin?

## Training Yourself to be Mentally Tough

### *Step One: Know What You Want*

To start with, you have to know what you want. You have to be able to picture it clearly in your mind. The first step is to make a clear, attainable goal. Define what being mentally tough looks like in context for you.

If you want to clean up your finances, maybe your mental toughness training for the week is making dinner every night instead of succumbing to ordering takeout. If your goal is to be more knowledgeable this year, commit to reading a book a week for the rest of the year. If you want to work on sharpening your self-discipline skills, work your schedule so you can fit in a good habit, like meditating or jogging. If you've been really bad lately about being present in your relationships, maybe your first step is deciding to leave your phone somewhere out of sight and spend half an hour with your spouse and your kids.

Notice how none of these tasks seem to be mountains you couldn't climb. The task itself doesn't have to be gigantic. The hard part is doing it consistently, every day, working at it even when you don't want to. There will be days you don't feel like cooking. Grit is grown by doing it when the motivation is at an all-time low, just because you know you should.

When creating these goals, keep in mind where your roadblocks will be. Make sure the tasks you create to accomplish your goals are built into your routine to become a habit. When you don't want to or don't feel like showing up, accomplishing your task out of habit will save you. Remember that being mentally tough isn't about what feels good. It's about sticking to the schedule regardless of how you feel about it. It's about being consistent with your habits and your routine to get to your goal. That's what's going to set you apart. Every day when you complete your task, be sure to celebrate your progress and your wins. Every step you take is getting you closer to the person you want to be.

## *Step Two: Tweak Your Self-Talk*

Your brain is a powerful machine, and it's constantly working. Whether you realize it or not, you say 300 to 1,000 words per minute to yourself. What do they sound like? It might not seem like a big deal when you mutter, "Oh, that was stupid," to yourself after making a mistake, or, "Yikes, that could've gone better," when you bomb a presentation. But for Navy SEALs, self-talk can mean the difference between passing or failing. Welcome to the Pool Comp.

The Pool Competency Test is all about staying calm and positive when everything around you threatens danger. Imagine this: you're underwater, decked out in scuba gear. Everything is normal, in the surreal kind of way the world feels underwater. Suddenly, the equipment feeding oxygen to your mouth is ripped out, and the tube filling oxygen to that mouthpiece is tied in a knot.

If we went into this exercise cold-turkey, without any training, our hearts would be racing. This is a matter of life and death. You have to get your equipment back under control. But your hands are shaking, your mind is racing, and your heart rate won't relax for an instant. Panic sets in. Game over.

While our challenges might not be pool competency tests, this is a great example of how training your mind to be tough can affect how you behave, react, and get after your goals. The SEALs who were able to think rationally and positively about their outcomes while their lives were at stake were the ones who passed the exam, and also the ones who have the greatest mental toughness.

Outside of possibly saving your life, studies show that being positive is actually beneficial in many ways. Gratitude is proven to cause an increase in happiness, which is no surprise, considering gratitude is a self-discipline that makes us see the world around us positively.

Positivity can also be infectious in your relationships. A term called social optimism states that merely believing that people will like you will actually make people like you more. Optimism can benefit you at work by creating more opportunities for you, just because your positive mindset is sure you can achieve them.

Tweaking your self-talk towards positivity sounds easy and straight-forward enough, but so many of us have negative self-talk already programmed into our brains as a habit. You have to rewire yourself to think positively. Start by coming up with truthful affirmations for moments of panic and anxiety. Pessimism tends to tell you that bad things last forever, are universal, and mean you're a horrible person. Here's an example.

Another candidate gets the job you've been working for the past year to earn. Pessimism tells you this bad thing will last forever. Your mind might say, "I'm never going to leave this office." Instead, tell yourself the truth: bad things pass. "I am going to get a better position. It's just not happening this time."

Similarly, pessimism will tell you that bad things are universal. You walk out to the parking lot of the grocery store and find that your car's been hit, just in time to watch a teenager peel out of the parking lot and onto the adjacent street.

Fuming, you're probably thinking, "This would happen to me today! Things like this always happen to me!" Instead of digging yourself into a rut of self-pity, change your thoughts. Bad things have specific causes and don't just happen to you. Bad things are not universal.

The last place your mind tends to wander when it's in danger is to blame yourself. You finally got that new job you've been gunning for, but it's really difficult. Even in training, your new position requires a lot of concentration and study to understand. Everything is unfamiliar. You might trudge home thinking, "I'm worthless. I can't do this." But is that the truth? No. The truth is that you're struggling with a new skill. You are not terrible at this job just because you're struggling with it.

Another tool to battle pessimism is to argue with yourself. If your brain is telling you something negative, use a mental model like Elon Musk's First Principles to dig to the root of the negativity. If the thought is, "I'll never be a good dad," question why you think that. Is it because you don't have much experience in childcare? Is it because you'd like to be different from your dad and you're not sure how to do that?

Come up with a logical counter-argument, based in fact instead of emotion (like your original negative thought probably is). Suddenly, "I'll never be a good dad," turns into, "I don't have much experience with children, but if I work at it, I can have good relationships with children." If you decide, your negative thought is one that needs to be countered even further, make it a point to create goals that will strengthen your counter-argument. Offer to babysit for your friends or a family member. Ask for help from a mom or a dad, and talk to them about your fears.

Often, positivity is a skill that's overlooked because it's seen as less-than. People think of being positive as a piece of fluff to fill another line on the "special skills" section on your resume. The ever-faster, better, and stronger working monologue that's been ground into our brains says that any tool you can't use physically isn't worth using.

The truth about positivity, however, is that it's something much greater than we give it credit for. Some people are naturally positive. It doesn't take much for them to see something beautiful in the wreckage. Others struggle with this skill. Either way, strengthening it does more benefit for your health, for your future work, and your relationships.

What you'll start to realize as you practice positivity is that it's infectious. People will start to notice that you are "the happy person" or "the bright-side person," and they'll flock to you. Bosses want positive people on their teams. Potential boyfriends and girlfriends want positive people to love and love them. Your friends will start to catch the drift and develop a more positive perspective, too. When you look up, your life looks up.

Another tangible practice you can use to think more positively is to keep a gratitude journal. If you've been in the realm of personal growth long, you've heard this one a million times. That's because it works. Writing down things you're glad to have actually trains your mind to look for things that make your life as good as it is.

The change is slight at first. You might not recognize it after the first day, or even the first week, but it's there. In the back of your mind when you're struggling with pessimism, a little grateful voice will remind you of something good.

You can almost feel yourself getting a little lighter every time you write another thing or another person you're thankful is around. For the million and first time, consider keeping track of the things you're grateful for. Maybe that can be your new habit.

To sum it up:

1. Know what you want. Set a goal that's clear and attainable. Create new habits that will lead you to these goals.

2. Tweak your self-talk. Don't underestimate the power of positivity (or the power of pessimism).

Next up, we'll talk about some habits that mentally tough people put in place in their lives. Maybe you'll find one or two you already adhere to, or maybe you'll a couple that need to make a home in your schedule.

## Habits of Mentally Tough People

1. They surround themselves with people who think differently than them (especially if those different thinkers remind them of someone they want to be like).

Being around people who have had different experiences, different upbringings, or different areas of competence is a lesson in getting out of your comfort zone. We like to be comfortable. We like to stay in the realm of confidence, where we can predict what will happen next, and what we will do when it happens.

Being around people who lead different kinds of lives than you will open your eyes to situations you wouldn't run into on your own path. We all have different stories, different beliefs, and different dreams, and hearing about someone else's may just expand your own or awaken a passion you didn't know you had.

2. They engage in simulations of situations that terrify them.

How would you feel if right now, without any warning, you received a phone call for your dream job, and all you had to do was an interview for it in the next two minutes? Are your hands sweating just thinking about it? Even more than death, the number-one fear in America is oral communication. Simply verbally communicating under pressure is enough to make most of the United States tremble.

If you're one of the millions, and you hate interviews, wouldn't you like to make that experience a little easier?

Simulating that terrifying situation can help. Conducting mock-interviews with family members and friends can help you to rehearse well-thought answers to typical interview questions.

When your future boss asks what your worst working trait is, you won't fumble over your words or laugh nervously if you've been over it a few times. Consider simulating the experience a trial run. The more trial runs you rehearse of a situation that scares you, the more confident you will be in that situation (and the less it will scare you).

3. They prepare.

True story: once on my first day at a new job, I forgot one of my shoes. I was running late that morning and threw both my shoes and my jacket into the passenger seat and took off for the office at a scary speed. I peeled into the parking lot, grabbed the keys out of the ignition, and went to put on my shoes, only to realize that only one of them was lying on the passenger seat.

I began a mad search for his brother. It wasn't under the passenger seat. It wasn't in between the seat and the console. It wasn't in the backseat. I started the morning fifteen minutes late, after limping into the nearest store with one shoe on my foot to buy new shoes. Later that night, I found my shoe on the floor of the garage, where it must have slipped out of my ill-prepared hands and onto the concrete slab.

The moral of the story is this: if I had woken up ten minutes earlier that morning and thought through the challenges of the day and fully prepared myself mentally for them, I probably would've shown up with both shoes on.

Preparing for the challenges ahead, both mentally and physically, will make you feel more confident and organized, put you at ease, and lend you a clearer, less emotional mind. You'll probably be wearing two shoes, too.

4. They are creative.

You are less likely to freeze under pressure if you already practice being creative and adaptable in your day-to-day life. Planning is great and needs to happen to prepare you for situational outcomes, but there will always be a kink in the plan.

There will always be something that doesn't go as it should have. In those instances, you will have to be creative and flexible to work around them. Great mothers and nannies do this phenomenally.

The plan may be to go to the park. Mom or babysitter has the baby backpack chock-full of tools for the day ahead because they planned for it. However, children are bundles of joy and surprises, so when the unthinkable happens, and little Johnny jumps straight into the water fountain, the caretaker has to be creative. Because she planned for the unexpected, she has an extra set of clothes for little Johnny.

However, when he then rolls around in the mud in his new set of clothes, mom or babysitter will have to adapt their mindset. Little Johnny might get carted home in a new diaper and not much else. Just like in this example, sometimes the key to creativity and adaptability doesn't require much else than a change of expectation.


5. They engage in physical exercise to stretch themselves (both physically and mentally).

I know what you're thinking: what does achieving mental toughness have to do with how many times a week I go to the gym? Physical exercise is one of the most popular and easiest ways to engage mental toughness.


Remember gym class in high school, when your teacher made you run laps around the gym? When your lungs burned, and your legs felt like jello, you kept running, partially because your classmates would all see if you stopped, and partially because you wanted to see if you could.

You were training yourself to be mentally tough. Now, as an adult, that manifests like this: doing five reps instead of just doing four. Getting up out of bed and going for a run when you really just want to sleep in the extra thirty minutes.

Pushing yourself to run to that lamppost, and then the next one. The relationship between pushing your body and pushing your mind is strong.

6. They balance their time between training and resting.

Don't mistake mental toughness practice for lack of balance between your goals and rest. Mental toughness isn't devoting all your time and energy, all the time, to attaining your goals. It's about being hyper-focused and persistent in the time you've allotted to work toward your goals. Going full-power all the time will lead to burn-out and stress, neither of which is helpful for growing your mental toughness.

Tips for Mental Toughness:

- When you're struggling with being creative, break out of your normal day-to-day routine. Do something different.

- Use the scenario analysis mental model to start your day. Mentally rehearsing for challenges that may come up will ensure that you are more prepared when these situations do occur.

- Picture yourself achieving your goals and how you will get there. Be honest and realistic in these visualizations. Leave room for setbacks.

- Write your goals down and track your progress. Few things are more motivating than being able to see tangibly how you're moving closer to where you want to be.

- If you end up missing a day or two of your new habit, don't make excuses for yourself and don't beat yourself up. Just get back into it as soon as you can.

- Again, celebrate your victories!

What can you do today to start becoming more mentally tough? Do you know what you want or do you need to sit down and prioritize your goals using some of the mental models we've discussed? Do you know what tasks or habits you want to introduce to your daily routine to accomplish your goals? Do you have an accountability partner who will call you out when you don't accomplish that task?

You can be a person with grit. Your success is up to you and how hard you're willing to work for it. Leave behind the misconception that you're not talented enough or experienced enough, and start believing this: you are already on your way to where you want to end up.

# Chapter 5: Using Mental Models to Achieve Stoicism

One of the defining qualities of being human is the vast array of emotions we feel. We respect people who are empathetic, or understanding of others' emotions, and elevate them to extreme pedestals. We study famous artists in school who use canvases and sculpting clay to express their emotions, and we call it beautiful. We watch movies and root for the characters we like best because they display appropriate emotions at appropriate times. In customer service, we love to be asked how we're doing or how our day is going. Because we want to talk about our feelings.

The truth about our feelings is that they're messy, complicated, and sometimes over-exaggerated. Sometimes they're present and so overwhelming that we have no idea how to name them or why they're there.

For many, emotions rule the world. They guide decisions, relationships, and futures. They find themselves on an emotional roller coaster throughout the day, reacting to whatever challenges or joys arise and allowing them to define their emotional state.

Emotions are fickle and mercurial. They can change at a moment's notice. Even so, many people have fallen prey to their emotions. But there's hope for you, even if your emotions are out of control, because you're here, reading this. The trick is to figure out how to control your emotions internally without allowing the world to change your mind.

Traditionally, the word 'stoic' brings to mind bland and even negative pictures. We think of stoic people as unfeeling, or inhuman. We think of dark, lost souls without any joy. But stoicism is actually the practice of controlling your emotions, not getting rid of them.

Stoicism is a belief system that states you can't control your external situation. Stoics believe the entire world is a web of cause and effects, called logos, neither of which we can control. You can't snap your fingers and make the morning commute traffic disappear. You can't crank back the clock and break off that awful relationship a month earlier when it should've been. What you can control, however, is how you react to your external situation, and whether you will allow it to affect you.

This is the basis stoicism is built on. Stoics recognize that most of the time, we can control neither the causes nor the effects of the world around us, so they seek to improve themselves while watching on as the world spins on without our input. They use four different pillars to realize better self-discipline and maturity: practical wisdom, courage, justice, and temperance.

Practical wisdom is the ability to look at emotional and complicated situations and steer through them using logic and information, calmly.

Courage refers to the virtue of facing challenges with integrity and bravery.

The third pillar, justice, means that stoics believe in treating everyone, regardless of worth to their journey or elevation in life, with equal kindness.

Finally, temperance is the discipline of utilizing moderation and self-control in any area of life.

The history of stoicism is a surprisingly lengthy one, beginning about two thousand years ago in Athens in third century B.C. It was founded by Zeno of Citium but made popular by the thinkers Marcus Aurelius and Epictetus, among many others.

Marcus Aurelius was the emperor of the Roman Empire, and the author of a series of thoughts called The Meditations. These scripts held impressive tips to become more stoic in everyday life, some of which we'll examine here based on quotes from his text.

Marcus Aurelius: Thoughts on Stoicism

*"Ask yourself at every moment- is this necessary?"*

*-Marcus Aurelius*

You have a limited amount of time and a limited amount of energy you can use every single day. You get to choose how you spend those precious resources. Aurelius teaches that if the answer to this question at any point is no, you might be wasting time or energy that could be useful elsewhere. Develop a list of priorities to focus on, and devote your energy and time to those necessary things.

*"Labor willingly and diligently, undistracted, and aware of the common interest."*

*-Marcus Aurelius*

This quote from Aurelius is all about discipline. Self-discipline is necessary to continue working toward your goals, totally focused, but another kind of self-discipline presents itself in the stoic arena. This kind of self-discipline Aurelius refers to is the discipline of your thoughts and emotions. You could be devoting full energy to completing a task when suddenly, you're blind-sided by stressful thoughts.

It occurs to you that your car payment is due on the thirteenth of the month and you're not sure how you're going to pay it on time. Another thought flies in on its curtails: you should go back to school. You should start scholarship applications soon. Suddenly, your mind is totally inundated by stressful thoughts about external situations that unmoor you from your train of thought and your task completion.

Don't allow outside stressful thoughts to distract you from the task at hand and the energy you're devoting to it. If the things you're stressing about are in your control, write them down to deal with them later. If they're not, confront and accept them and move on.

*"Never shirk the proper dispatch of your duty, no matter if you are freezing or hot, groggy or well-rested, vilified or praised, not even if dying or pressed by other demands."*

*-Marcus Aurelius*

This quote is a perfect summary of the stoic school of thought. Once you have a singular focus on what you want to achieve, employing a mindset of stoicism means you accept the sacrifice of not bowing to every emotional need. We are so used to catering to our needs and making ourselves completely comfortable that we think it's a necessity for success. Aurelius is saying that our comfort is totally unnecessary to our success, and our success is worth the sacrifice.

## Epictetus: Thoughts on Stoicism

Epictetus was a Greek philosopher who famously began as a slave. He is best known for an integral idea of stoicism called the dichotomy of control, which one of Marcus Aurelius' main ideas already alluded to.

The idea behind the dichotomy of control is that we recognize the difference between which things are within our control, and which aren't. Once we recognize those differences, we accept it, come to terms with it, and move on. Here are some famous teachings from Epictetus, guided by his own words.

*"Make a practice at once of saying to every strong impression: 'An impression is all you are, not the source of the impression.' Then test and assess it with your criteria, but primarily, ask: 'Is this something that is, or that is not, in my control?'"*

*-Epictetus*

The first idea Epictetus proposes to us is to recognize our 'impressions', or our first reaction to things (which is usually emotional, not logical).

The dichotomy of control asks that when situations occur, we step back from our original emotional reaction and allow logic to come into play so we can assess whether or not we can control the outcome. As difficult as this sounds, if we conclude that the outcome is out of our control, all we can do is ignore it and not allow it to affect us.

For example, say your boss comes to you frustrated in the middle of the workday. He spends five minutes talking to you, red in the face and then storms out of your office.

A couple of minutes later, you realize that the situation he was so upset about has nothing to do with your department and isn't something that your actions could enhance or make worse. At that moment, it's up to you whether you'll allow your boss's mid-day rant to make you grumpy for the rest of the workday.

On the other hand, you could employ a tactic from the stoic school of thought, take a deep breath, and continue about your day, ignoring the complicated situation you have no control over.

*"When giving your child or wife a kiss, repeat to yourself: 'I am kissing a mortal.'"*

*-Epictetus*

The second value we learn from Epictetus is to value the impermanence of things. Although this seems morose and depressing out of context, Epictetus is right.

The world is fickle, and life ebbs and flows however it pleases. The beautiful things we have today could be gone tomorrow. At any moment, something out of your control could come and take away the things that are most dear to you.

Families are affected by natural disasters, like hurricanes and floods, where their houses are completely washed away. Communities like Squirrel Hill in Pittsburgh and so many others are totally decimated by shootings in local worship centers and schools.

None of these things could be planned for or controlled. The day before disaster struck was just another normal day. Epictetus is urging us to consider that as horrible as it is, this could be our fate, too.

He's saying to find incredible joy and appreciation by never taking it for granted that you could be kissing your loved one for the last time, or talking to your mom on the phone for the second-to-last time. Remember the total mortality of those you love, and you will appreciate your life with them even more.

*"Whenever planning an action, mentally rehearse what the plan entails."*

*-Epictetus*

Next, we learn that bad things don't just happen to bad people, and we should plan accordingly.

Make goals that are within your control. If you ultimately want to be a famous singer on the radio or television, you have to accept that standing alone, fame is not a goal that you can say without a doubt is totally within your control. What you can control, however, is attaining the goal that will lead to your ultimate goal of fame.

Continuing to use our superstar-singer example, this lead-up goal could be to rehearse an incredible setlist for an open mic night to gain performance practice. Another attainable goal to achieve your final outcome could be to audition for a singing show.

Once you've made a lead-up goal that is within your realm of control, the idea is to accept any possible outcome could occur. If you audition for a televised singing show, the judges could love you and ultimately, you could be given a record deal. However, another outcome you have to consider is that your audition will be outright rejected.

Yet another outcome is that you'll make it on the show, only to get kicked off a week later and come back to square one. Bad things don't just happen to bad people, and by mentally preparing for those outcomes, you can get a head-start on accepting the feelings that will come with them.

Preparing yourself for all of these possible outcomes and preparing for goals that you can control will lead you down a much more stoic and emotionally stable path.

This will also keep you motivated to get up and try again if the outcome you hoped for doesn't come to fruition. So many times, we put the best effort forward for goals we don't have control over, and then when we fail, we blame ourselves. We tie our strong efforts to that failure and begin to think that we are failures when this isn't the case at all.

You have to set yourself up for success by shooting for goals that are attainable and continuing to meet those goals until you get where you ultimately want to be. This idea comes from the first pillar of stoicism, wisdom.

Logic says that even if you deserved whatever you wanted- the promotion or the adopted child or the better treatment, or whatever you'd love to have- sometimes the prized outcome isn't the one that comes true. Logic says that you might deserve what you want and not get it anyway.

This school of thought is generally perceived as a dark one. It involves accepting that things won't be golden all the time and basically tells its' adherents to quash hope in exchange for reality. However, stoics are generally more content and more self-disciplined.

They're also more emotionally stable because their moods don't swing up and down depending on the rhythm of the day. If you struggle with allowing your emotions to take control of your life, just trying a stoic approach for a week, or a couple of weeks, might make a difference in your life.

Let's learn about a couple of mental models you can try to approach stoicism in a more tangible way.

# Commitment and Consistency Bias

"*Mom!* I can't find my shoes!"

It's 4:20 pm and mom and daughter are already running late for cheer practice when this exclamation rings down the staircase to the mothers' ears. Sighing, she begins upending couch cushions as she yells back.

"Have you checked under your bed?"

"Yes!"

"In your closet?"

"*Yes,* mom!"

"Are you *sure* you checked under your bed?"

A path of stomping feet shakes the ceiling above as the daughter makes her way to the top of the staircase.

"I *told* you, I *checked!*"

Stomping back to her room, the daughter lowers herself onto her belly to check one last time under the bed skirt. This time, her eyes spot the white soles of a Reebok cheer sneaker. Feeling her face heat up, she glances toward the door, and then back at the shoe. Grabbing the laces, she shoves it further back under the bed and tugs the pink silk bed skirt back down.

"I can't find them," she yells down the stairs again, "I'll just wear my running shoes and find them later!" Still blushing, she pulls on her tennis shoes and flies out the door, down the stairs, and into the van. Her mom will never know she was wrong.

At one point or another, we've all been guilty of a situation like this. We know we're wrong, but we've insisted we're right. We don't want to be found out, so we bury the evidence and assert our innocence. No matter what, our pride- and the consistency and confirmation bias- tell us no one can know. It's this mental model that makes us cover our tracks.

The confirmation and consistency bias mental model is emotion-based, not logic-based. This is why understanding it and recognizing its' presence in our own lives is so important to practicing stoicism. This mental model, defined, is our desire to protect our self-image. We want to appear to everyone around us that we are consistent in our behaviors and beyond any setbacks, that we will maintain this commitment to be consistent.

Whether we realize it or not, we have a thing about consistency. We all have that 'flaky' friend or family member that the group has labeled inconsistent. They can't be trusted to show up for their commitments. They're unpredictable, emotional, and hard to trust. None of us want to be thought of this way.

Instead, we want to appear committed. We want to be the one our boss can count on to get the big project done, and done well, even if behind the scenes, we're all up night stressing about it. We want our friends to think we're the ones that will be there for them at any hour of the night, even if it exhausts us. It's worth that social media caption on our birthday: 'they're the one I can *always* count on.'

But here's the thing: if you want to try out the stoic side of life, you have to acknowledge these feelings and then let them go. All the worries about how people think of you have to disappear. If you want to be freed from the shackles of your emotions, it starts here: with figuring out how the commitment and consistency bias has taken root in you.

The first key component to understanding the commitment and consistency bias is public action. The more public your affirmation, the stronger your commitment to it is. Accountability works because this mental model is at the core of it. For example, if you set a goal to lose thirty pounds but don't tell anyone, you can give up on the goal in a week without achieving it without getting any gall from anyone else besides yourself.

However, if you tell four friends when you decide to embark on this weight loss journey, they'll follow up with you and ask how it's going. If you decide to quit, you have to deal with them: what they think of you for telling them to hold you accountable and then giving up. The power of that shame is strong enough that you'll probably continue on the weight loss journey simply because you don't want to let them down. You don't want them to think you're inconsistent, or not a person of your word.

The next aspect of this mental model that makes it so strong is the amount of effort that's put in. The more effort you expend on a project or idea, the stronger your commitment to it is. You're more committed to a project on day one hundred after you've spent time, money, and energy on it than you are on day one.

So how do you slay this commitment and consistency bias once and for all? The first step, of course, is awareness. Sit down and think about which relationships, and which areas of your life, this mental model is affecting. Where is the urge strongest to impress people? Who do you want most to think you're consistent and reliable?

When your mother calls, is it really important for you to stress how well you're doing? Do you subliminally (or obviously) let her know at some point in the conversation that your life is great, your finances have never been better, and you love your job? Your relationship with your mom might be tainted with the commitment and consistency bias.

When your boss asks for another favor, even you're already swamped, do you take it with a smile and move it to the top of your priority list? That action might be powered by commitment and consistency bias.

What about the in-laws? Does the mere thought of sitting down at the dinner table alone with them while your significant other uses the restroom make you sweat? Consider that relationship for hints of the commitment and consistency bias.

Once you've determined which relationships make you cling to your self-image, you can be more aware of the conversations and actions that ensue. Being aware of when you're most vulnerable will help you to learn where you have to be most strong. Wait until your mom asks about your finances if she even does.

As difficult as it may be, slow down and be honest with your boss about your full plate. They'll respect you even more for having the self-awareness and discipline to say no. When your significant other scoots back their chair to head to the restroom, take a deep breath and remember that they like you for who you are, not for who you make their parents think you are. In any case, this is a mental model that will take time and discipline to abolish.

Tips for Abolishing the Commitment and Consistency Bias:

- Don't ignore assessing your emotions. When reaching for stoicism, it's really tempting to ignore emotions entirely. However, that's not what this school of thought is asking you to do at all. Assess and accept your emotions about how you want others to see you. The only way to get rid of this bias is by working through it.

- Use this bias in your favor. When you're nervous about starting a new habit, use accountability partners to keep you going. As long as you recognize that their opinion of you isn't the point here, utilizing this mental model for your success is brilliant.

- Fight the urge to be right. Pride will only land you in an ugly place.

## Cognitive Appraisal

When was the last time you said, "That made me feel like..." or "She/he/they made me feel like..."? My guess is, you probably said something along those lines at least once already either today or yesterday. It is ingrained in our nature and our language to think that other people and their actions are responsible for our emotions.

You're standing in line at the grocery store at the six o'clock hour. The place is teeming with last-minute dinner preppers. All around you, grumpy, end-of-the-workday shoppers are giving each other looks, snatching items off of shelves, and pushing their carts in huffs past people who are taking too long.

You're finally the next person up in the self-checkout line, and your basket is starting to wear a strange angular imprint on your forearm where the handle has been resting. The stressed-out attendant smiles at you from her computer screen as another shopper leaves one of the kiosks, signaling that it's your turn to buy your groceries and get out of there.

Suddenly, an older gentleman walks right past you and sets his handheld cart down on the kiosk meant for you. Stunned, you blink and look at the attendant, who shrugs and continues to punch buttons on the screen in front of her. You feel the indignance rising. How dare he! It was your turn! You've waited all this time! It's not fair!

Right now, you could say that man who cut you in line is making you angry. It's ingrained in us, even in our language, to put the responsibility of our emotions on other people and external situations.

Think about it: when a situation arises, and we have an emotional response, what do we say? "She (or he) just *made me* so upset." We displace the emotional responsibility from ourselves to the other person involved in the situation that displeased us.

But back to the checkout line: you could say like anyone else would, that that man just made you so angry. But the truth is, what's actually creating that emotion rising in your chest is the way you perceived the situation and the thought process you used to land on your emotional response.

It's called Cognitive Appraisal. Apart from special circumstances where emotions really are caused directly by actions (breaking your leg, for example, causes pain), Cognitive Appraisal says that your emotions are your own responsibility.

Your feelings are derived directly from how you've appraised the situation before you. Others' actions and behaviors don't make us directly feel a certain way; it's our cognitive processes and beliefs that guide how we feel. This can feel a little unnerving because our language so strongly relates actions to our emotions.

"My brother was mean to me, so I am sad."

"My car broke down, so I am frustrated."

"That man cut me in line at the grocery store, so I am angry."

But this mental model actually theorizes that in any given situation, we can change how we feel by adapting our thought process. What's interesting about cognitive appraisal is that it occurs without us using it intentionally all the time, every time something stressful happens.

You come home from work one day to find that the dog has dug a hole under the fence in the backyard and escaped. Your mind will immediately begin to go through the first phase of cognitive appraisal: primary appraisal.

During primary appraisal, your brain asks, "How will this stressor impact me?" In this case, your dog being lost means you will have to go out and look for him. The plans you made to settle in on the couch with a glass of wine and an awful episode of reality tv are gone. If you don't find him, the impact on you will be the loss of your pet.

Secondary appraisal begins not long after primary appraisal. It takes into account all the information the primary appraisal concluded and develops your emotional response based on that information. Realizing you might not have a dog anymore might make you sad.

The recognition that you will now spend what would've been a relaxing night at home on the streets searching for your dog might trigger a frustrated response. In any case, as you run out the front door yelling your dog's name with treats in hand, you have unwittingly gone through the cognitive appraisal process to land at an emotional response.

Now that you're aware of this mental model, you can start to use it logically to change your thought process and response. In the grocery store, when the older man cut in front of you, your first reaction was an emotional one. Feelings took over because the thought process wasn't intentional. Let's use the cognitive appraisal mental model to think through this example.

What is the personal impact of someone cutting in front of you in the grocery store line? You will be in the grocery store for a few more minutes until someone else at another register finishes up their purchases, and you can use their checkout machine. Feelings aside, this is really the only logical impact that will occur because the man cut in front of you.

Based on this information, choosing to be frustrated about an action that will only impact the next five or ten minutes of your night seems cavalier. On the other hand, you could choose to take a deep breath and allow calmness to come over you instead. In the next few minutes, the checkout attendant will again sheepishly smile at you and motion you toward another vacant machine. Life will go on.

You might be reading this and thinking, "But the point isn't that his action will only physically affect the next ten minutes of my life. The point is that I am just as important as that man, and his actions didn't make it seem that way."

Although this is a fair assessment, and a valid issue to have, the dichotomy of control model asks us to consider what about this situation we can control. We can control our own reaction.

We can control how we treat others; like they're just as important as us. However, we can't control the actions of other people, and there's nothing we could have done to control the actions of the stranger in the grocery store.

The stoic philosophy would say that because you cannot control the outcome of that situation, you should ignore it and not allow it to affect your day. Similarly, stoicism would say you can't derive your worth from the external world. Don't allow one stranger's actions to be enough to make you feel less-than.

Tips for Using Cognitive Appraisal:

- When you're faced with situations like the grocery store example, think through each feeling that arises before you cast it aside. Use the dichotomy of control principle to ask yourself, "Is this something I can do something about? Or is this something I have to let go?"

- Try not to get hung up on principles. You're right; sometimes it *is* about the principle of the thing: people shouldn't cut in line. But ask yourself: will starting a confrontation make you more or less content in the end?

- Train yourself to slow down your reaction time. Remember that the more thorough you are in using this mental model, the less mess you'll have to clean up later.

- You can practice using cognitive appraisal during meditation, or even during your scenario analysis of the day. Think through the challenges of the day and how you'll respond to each one.

## *More Practices for Stoicism from Seneca*

Seneca the Younger, also known as just Seneca, was a Roman philosopher and is a big name is Stoicism. These are additional tangible practices to achieve stoicism in your day-to-day life, as told by his teachings.


1.  Practice wanting.

Seneca asserts that it was essential to his mental health as a stoic is to take a couple of days out of the month and live in poverty.


On these impoverished days, he would wear older, dirty clothes, eat smaller meals, and deny himself small joys that on an ordinary day, he would indulge in. By doing this exercise, he put himself face-to-face with what most people are terrified of most: being without.


He faced and conquered this fear head-on by proving to himself that at the end of the day, he was still alive. This practice also reinforces the stoic concept that happiness isn't derived from the outside world; it's something you create within yourself.


2. Train yourself to think there's no "good" or "bad."

We have been told since childhood that there is a "good" side and a "bad" side. "Good" guys and "bad" guys. "The good witch" and "the wicked witch of the west." However, words like good and bad are entirely subjective. Perception is everything. This is why you should wipe those words out of your vocabulary.


There's no such thing as good or bad- just the way you perceive a situation as better or worse for you. "Bad" things can easily be turned on their heads with logic to become lessons. "Good" things are fickle and can easily fade or become a "bad" thing when too much is vested in it. Do away with these subjective words and see things for the way they are.


3. Use the birds-eye-view approach.

The world is a big and beautiful place. It's incredible to think about how many people are all alive, all at once, all living totally different lives. People are getting up for work at the same time other people are tucking in to go to sleep.

People on one side of the world are having babies and others on the other side of the world are watching their grandparents pass away. Some people might've landed their dream job today, while others were laid off.

This is using the birds-eye-view approach. Looking at your own little life in the context of millions of others makes you realize not only how small you are, but how good your life is. Things could be completely opposite for you right now because somewhere in the world, someone is living that life.

The things that bring you joy could be the things someone else is mourning. You are so overwhelmingly blessed, and you'll see it better through this lens.

4. Continue to use the dichotomy of control.

One of the most integral keys for using the stoic system is releasing your grip on control. A lot of us have control issues. We like to know what to expect, so we know how to plan, so everything goes smoothly and without a hitch. Live like that for long, though, and you'll start to notice something: the world is full of hitches.

No matter how tightly you cling to that plan or try to weasel your way into controlling something (or someone) else to go your way, there will always be a hitch. It is so much easier to simply take a deep breath and let go. There are still things you can control the heck out of. But some things, you just won't be able to.

We live in an overdramatic, over-emotional world. We are asked from day one how we are doing. Everyone is a little bit more sensitive as the years go on.

We crave emotional understanding and believe emotional intelligence is a kind of superpower. Feelings are beautiful, and they strengthen relationships and help us interact with one another. But their place in our lives is not at the helm of the ship.

So many of us live on emotional roller coasters. We get home at the end of the day and when the one who loves us asks, "how was your day," it's no longer a one-word answer. We have to take a moment to recap all of the exciting, emotional events that plunged us into despair or had us riding an emotional high.

It's exhausting, isn't it? To live a life where anything can change at a moment's notice. At the mouth of a co-worker talking behind your back. At the praise of your boss during a meeting and then the cafe's lack of oat milk in the next thirty minutes.

Stoicism may seem cold to our soft, emotional beings, but it is a kind of freedom. We live shackled to the way we feel. We think we have no control over the breaks in the waves, but we do, and we have no idea how to captain our own ship. Stoicism paves the way for deciding for yourself that your future is going to be bright, and you're going to make it that way.

Stoicism is the path that says, "This is what I'm doing, and nothing can stop me, no matter what annoying inconvenience comes next to ruin me."

If you want to put your hands on the wheel of your life, of your success, of your future, you should try being the captain for a change. You should try deciding how you're going to feel and then feeling that way. Welcome to a stoic lifestyle.

# Chapter 6: Building Your Own Mental Model

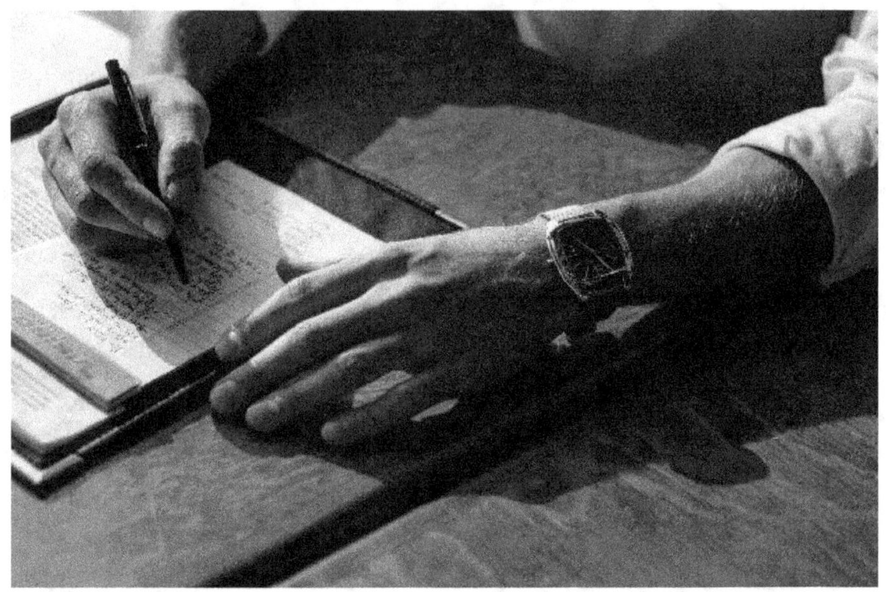

As you've probably already guessed, there are mental models that work better for some people and mental models that work better for others. For some, the Circle of Competency mental model might strike a chord and change the whole trajectory of their life. Another person might read about the same mental model and not feel affected at all.

We each have a unique mindset, learning style, and goal, which means we each need a different combination of mental models to get us there. Mental models are a unique tool in that you can pick and choose which models pair together well to accomplish your individual goals. You can even construct your own worldview to add to the mix.

Developing your own toolkit of mental models, or even building your own mental model, will work best to achieve your goals because the more individualized your tools, the greater they will work for your individual outcome.

Building a mental model might seem like a daunting task. So far, we've seen billionaire investors, inventors, athletes, and even Navy SEALs coming up with, and using, their own mental models. But you don't have to be famous, worth billions, or even brilliant, to design a mental model that will work specifically and uniquely for your purposes in your life.

We're going to break down this project into a definition, a series of steps, and a list of tips. Before you know it, you'll be lumped along with the businessmen worth billions and the spaceship phenomenons.

We'll start by renaming what a mental model is. After five chapters of nothing but examples of mental models, the actual, technical definition might have snuck out the backdoor.

Remember that a mental model is simply an image of the world as you see it that affects the way you make decisions and react to it. It's a simple concept that can expand to include self-discipline, work habits, and other important tactics to accomplish your goals.

## Identifying Your Mental Models and Their Impacts

Now that you know a little bit more about mental models after reading this book, you'll want to start by identifying the mental models that you currently operate with. Like we mentioned earlier in this book, you've probably been operating with mental models all your life without knowing it.

How you were raised has a big impact on how you see the world, even as an adult. Many stereotypes are built from childhood. For example, if a family member you grew up close to was homophobic, you might have a harder time accepting the LGBTQ+ community as an adult. For most of your childhood, you saw this family member wrinkle their nose when two girls kissed on a television show or use the word 'gay' as an insult. It will take recognition, time, and work for you to rewrite the worldview your family member has written for you about homosexual relationships.

Take a close look at the values of your parents and the values of your family. What are the topics that come up in conversation frequently? When your dad calls or stops by to ask how you're doing, what kind of questions does he ask?

My parents started their family young. When they began having children, neither of them had the life skills necessary to run a household. Soon, they realized that money ran out quickly when you didn't budget or save, but neither of them knew how to rectify the situation between working and taking care of kids. The result was a cycle of living paycheck-to-paycheck, riding the high on payday and then dramatically plummeting into poverty as the money ran out toward the end of the month.

In her mid-thirties, my mom finally got sick of this lifestyle, and her worldview about finances turned the opposite direction, into almost obsession. Now when she calls, she asks about how my savings account is doing. In an outreach of love, she'll ask if I want her to look over my budget for me. What makes her excited nowadays is a really good sale at the grocery store or the outlet store.

What is your worldview like about money? Are you a self-proclaimed "saver," plunking pennies down in jars on the counter? Do you keep a vigilant budget and know exactly where each dollar goes? Or are you more of a "spender," treating yourself to dinners out when you feel like it and getting a rush of intoxication come pay time?

Now turn your mind to your relationships. What is your mental model like when it comes to your family, your friends, your coworkers, and even strangers? What are your expectations like for others, and for yourself, in relationships? An interesting tool that may help you define your mental models when it comes to relationships are personality assessments like the Meyers-Briggs, Enneagram, DISC profile, or Five Love Languages.

The Meyers-Briggs test will assess you for your personality type based on four areas of life, resulting in a four-letter combination. You can read all about each of the letters on their website or in the subsequent results of your assessment.

The first letter will assess how you "recharge" best: whether you're more Introverted (I) or Extroverted (E). The second will assess how you view social situations: you'll either fall closer to the Intuition (N) side or the Sensing (S) side. The third letter will tell you when you make decisions if they're more likely to be Feeling-based (F) or Thinking-based (T). The fourth and final letter will tell you whether you like your world neat, organized, and predictable (Judging, noted with a 'J') or if you're a more go-with-the-flow person (Perceiving, 'P').

After finding your unique four-letter combination, this test will assign you a nickname based on the type and an in-depth assessment of how you tend to act in your personal relationships.

The Enneagram is a test based on the book 'The Road Back to You,' by Ian Morgan Cron and Suzanne Stabile. This test will assign you one number that will determine your personality type.

The DISC profile is a personality assessment geared toward working relationships. It will determine which of four personality types you fall under as a worker and how you relate to other workers of different personality types.

You might be a 'D' for Dominant, getting things done as bluntly and quickly as possible. You could be an 'I,' the bubbly, creative type that needs a push to get to the end of projects. You could be the slightly more introverted version of the 'I' personality, the 'S,' who is very sensitive but has excellent personal skills. Or, finally, you could be the 'C,' enjoying statistics and analysis and charts and graphs. The idea is that a team flourishes when it has an equal balance of all four personality types. The team will also flourish, however, if it knows which member is which type of the personality scale. For example, if you know you're an 'S,' and your boss is a 'D,' you can know that he'll come into your office without any small talk, grill you about a project deadline, and leave. Where before, this might have hurt your feelings and you might have thought hated you, you will be able to understand that 'D's operate on productivity and find joy in getting things done.

Similarly, if you're the boss in this situation and you know that your employee is an 'S,' you might start by asking how her cat is doing before launching into the tirade about the project schedule.

The final aptitude test mentioned here is the Five Love Languages, which is geared more towards personal or romantic relationships. This test will guide you in realizing how you feel most appreciated, and how you can make others feel the same way.

Even if you're devoting all of your energy to making your loved one feel appreciated, if you're not using their love language, it's not going to mean as much to them as it does to you. This test will file you into one of several categories: Words of Affirmation, Gifts, Physical Touch, Quality Time, or Acts of Service. Most of the time, how you demonstrate you love others is how you want to be shown you're loved back.

With that being said, if the most special thing to you is hearing someone verbally tell you how much you're appreciated, you're probably a Words of Affirmation adherent. Maybe you feel most loved when your boyfriend or girlfriend comes home with a surprise for you, even as simple as takeout for dinner or a bouquet of flowers.

You might be a Gifts person. If in the worst-case scenario, you've been known to be 'clingy,' but in the best-case scenario, you just like to be hugged and cuddled, you could be a person who values Physical Touch. The people who have the Quality Time love language really just need face-to-face, concentrated time. This means no phones, no other screens, just you and that loved one having a conversation or sitting side-by-side, enjoying each other without multi-tasking.

The final love language is for people who never feel more loved than when their family member or significant other recognizes they have a lot on their plate and decide to take something off of it for them. Mopping the kitchen floor while they're at work or prepping for dinner for the nights to come is the way to the heart for these people.

Each of these tests has a free version online that will test you for your aptitude or feelings on a variety of situations. Based on your answers, these tests will label you with an archetype based on their theory about personalities. Standing alone or comparing results from a multitude, none of the results from these tests should be taken as absolute truth.

Remember that they are all theories. When reading your results, think with a skeptical mind and glean information that feels true to you.

However, reading the results of personality tests like these is interesting to unveil ideas you might have about yourself and others you might not have noticed before. Each of these assessments will give you a different perspective on your romantic relationships, friendships, family relationships, and working relationships. You might be able to use some of that information to determine your worldview when it comes to these kinds of relationships.

You can also determine your mental models in relationships by simply observing the interactions you have with others and how your mind works during them. Do you often feel annoyed with your friend when she cancels plans at the last minute? You might have an expectation of commitment from your friend that differs from hers. If your girlfriend or wife is bugging you about how much you're on your phone lately, it might be because her love language is Quality Time and she needs some with you. If your daughter refuses to come out of her room, she might just be a teenager, or she might be recharging from a long day at school as an Introvert on the Meyers-Briggs scale.

## Expanding Your Mental Model

Now that you've determined which mental models you already use day-to-day, you can expand them to work better for you. Part of constructing your mental models toolkit is honing the mental models you already put into play. Use these steps to make your existing mental models work better for you.

1. LEARN.

Learn everything there is to know about your area of expertise, or your area of competency, as Charlie Munger would say. Read biographies and articles from the big-wigs of your world. Learn how they think and how they became successful. Learn to recognize their mental models (again, remember this is just a term for their worldview) and put them into play in your own life to see how they work for you.

## 2. LEARN MORE.

Studying the big names of your own practice is an excellent tool to gain new mental models, but also consider learning about other related, or even non-related fields. Look at successful companies and business owners, even if their products have nothing to do with your life. You're searching for attitudes and worldviews that make people successful, regardless of the business.

## 3. DISSECT YOUR OWN THOUGHTS.

Get into the habit of writing every day, or if you're not a writer, thinking out loud. The purpose of this exercise is to look at how you think and how putting new worldviews into place is affecting your ideas and thoughts. Keep track of these sessions in the notes app on your phone or in a notebook, even if it's just a bullet-point list. Constantly assess and reassess to judge how your mental models are doing.

## 4. PHONE A FRIEND.

Keeping your experiments with mental models in a vacuum will only usher in so much success. Every once in a while, you'll need new ideas and a new perspective. Tell a friend or a mentor, someone you respect, about the mental models you're trying out and how they're working for you. Ask them for feedback. What do they think? Do they see any unhealthy habits or perspectives forming? What do they think you could add to further deepen your perspective?

## 5. KEEP TABS ON YOUR OUTLOOK.

We learned in the last chapter that even when everything else is falling apart externally, we still get to control our emotions and our reactions. Being disciplined and focused on your goals will propel you forward, but even more so if you pair that motivation with a positive and level mindset. Keep practicing gratefulness and other stoic exercises we learned about to keep tabs on your mood and your mindset.

Now let's take a look at another mental model by the successful investor, Charlie Munger.

## The Lollapalooza Effect

For as linked as the term 'mental model' is with Charlie Munger's name, you would think that he's a psychology expert. However, mental models didn't always lie in Munger's area of competency. He actually got his start in understanding worldviews by reading several psychology textbooks as an adult, on his own. What he gleaned from his study of these textbooks is that we all operate with cognitive biases.

To refresh what we learned about cognitive biases in the first chapter, this term refers to any idea we have about the world that affects our behavior (and our success). At any given moment, we could be subject to one bias or another, but what Munger found is that when several cognitive biases coincided, they were more powerful than just one on its' own.

Munger calls this the Lollapalooza Effect, and it's a mental model. The most famous, and best example, Charlie Munger cites when he talks about this model is the Tupperware party. If you haven't heard of this, the

Tupperware party is an advertising technique much like a Pampered Chef or Mary Kay party. The seller of the product invites people to their home to demonstrate their wares and give an opportunity for their friends to purchase them. Munger asserts that this kind of advertising situation puts four different cognitive biases into play.

The first bias is Reciprocity. This cognitive bias says that when someone performs a favor for you or extends a kindness to you, you will have the urge reciprocate, or return the favor.

The second bias is Liking bias. This bias states that we like doing business with people we like, and therefore, we will conduct business interactions more often with people who are more like us.

The Social Proof bias is one we've already discussed. This bias operates in part with the bandwagon bias. To recap, the social proof bias means that if we're unsure about what to do, we will look around and do whatever the rest of the group is doing. When we're not confident about our actions, we follow suit with the rest of the crowd.

The final bias present in the Tupperware Party is another one we've already covered: the Commitment and Consistency bias. This was the bias where the daughter hid her cheer shoes further under the bed to maintain the idea that she was correct, rather than tell her mom she was wrong. The commitment and consistency bias states that even if we know we're wrong, we want so badly to appear consistent to others that we will resist changing our view.

Here's how it works in relation to the Tupperware Party. First, you get a call from your good friend Tom, who you're connected to in small but sure ways. Your kids went to elementary school together but are no longer friends. You work in the same building as his neighbor.

You see each other every once in a while in the grocery store and engage in small talk for a few minutes in the dairy aisle. So, Tom calls and invites you to a Tupperware party at his house the following Saturday.

Here comes liking bias: you like Tom and have no reason to blow him off, so you say, "Sure, why not, I'll go!"

The next Saturday comes and finds you in Tom's living room, sitting on Tom's couch, munching on Tom's Tupperware party snacks. The reciprocity bias starts to gnaw at you. Here is your friend, Tom, welcoming you into his home and extending this hospitality to you. Wouldn't it be rude if you came, accepted his hospitality, and left without buying any of his products? The reciprocity bias says you have to take home at least one thing from Tom's collection to pay him back for being so kind to you.

But which piece of Tupperware should you buy? After your friend's presentation, you find yourself at a loss. You know you have to take home something, but nothing really jumps out at you as something you need. You're totally unsure of your decision, but you see three or four people eyeing a Tupperware set over in the corner.

The social proof bias is upon you, and it says, "You don't know what to buy, but those people do. That Tupperware set must have value. I'll get that one!" Before you know it, you're headed home, a bag of Tupperware you probably didn't need in hand.

As you pull into the driveway, a sinking feeling settles into your gut. You picture the Tupperware cabinet in your kitchen, overflowing with discolored plastic bins and stacks of mismatching red and blue lids. You don't need any more Tupperware, and yet you went to a Tupperware party and brought some more home anyway.

Now whoever is on the other side of that door when you walk into the house is going to eye your new Tupperware and make fun of you for caving into the Tupperware party's schemes.

As you climb out of the car, grabbing your new Tupperware friends, you start to defend yourself in your head. You're in full commitment and consistency bias mode. Maybe you can get rid of some of the old Tupperware and replace it with the new stuff. You needed new Tupperware anyway.

These are high-quality containers. They'll last forever! On and on it goes as you march up the driveway, steeling yourself for the conversation to be had when you unlock the door and sneak inside with the Tupperware (let's be honest) you never really needed.

One by one, each of these cognitive biases probably wouldn't have gotten you into a situation like spending an afternoon with an acquaintance you don't really know out of obligation or sneaking into the house with Tupperware you don't really need. But together, this ensemble of cognitive biases completely derailed an entire Saturday afternoon and thirty dollars of your pocket money.

What the Lollapalooza Effect can tell us about building our own mental model is this: while one is strong, building a foundation of several overlapping mental models is much stronger. Though the Tupperware party is a classic example highlighting the nature of the Lollapalooza Effect, there are also positive ways this mental model can affect your life.

Take Alcoholics Anonymous, for example:

*"The system of Alcoholics Anonymous: a 50-percent no-drinking rate outcome when everything else fails? It's a very clever system that uses four or five psychological systems at once toward; I might say, a very good end."*

*-Charlie Munger*

When understood and used benevolently, a system of overlapping cognitive biases can create a powerful mental model used to urge you forward. If you know you're sensitive to the social proof bias (which states that when you're unsure, you'll do what everyone else is doing), you can surround yourself with people you look up to. That way, when you're subject to the social prof bias and find yourself flailing and copying someone else, you'll know it's at least a worthy decision.

Similarly, if you're aware that the reciprocity bias typically reels you in, you can live your life prepared to give willingly and generously. You might find that the key to desensitizing yourself to this bias is generous to someone before they have a chance to be kind to you. Going through life with that kind of a mindset can't steer you wrong.

Tips for Using the Lollapalooza Effect

- Be aware of the cognitive biases you're sensitive to. We've only studied a few of the many hundreds of kinds of biases in this book. Go online and research a list. One by one, make your way through the cognitive biases, thinking of how each could have a place in your life. If you're unaware of the biases you're subject to, you're leaving no room for change. Free yourself from the cognitive biases that might be holding you back.

- Study obligatory situations like the Tupperware party for cognitive biases that might be in play. If you find yourself thinking, "What am I doing here?" or, "This isn't how I wanted to spend my day (or my money)," you might be able to find a few cognitive biases hidden somewhere.

- Use these biases for good in your life! Manipulate yourself into sticking to your habits or running towards your goals by using the cognitive biases that seem to have the most presence in your life.

- Determine which mental models you can introduce cognitive biases into to make them even more powerful. Would the first principles model be easier for you to think through if you talked through it with someone you liked, using the liking bias? Would you be more motivated to complete an Eisenhower box if your friend checked in on you, using the commitment and consistency bias? Strengthen your toolkit by pairing your tools.

Before you started reading this book, you might not have known what mental models were. You might have heard the term before but not understood what they were. You might've done a little bit of research but not fully understood how to put them into place. Take a moment and congratulate yourself.

You have come so far from the person who opened this book for the first time. You now have the knowledge you can apply practically any time you choose in any area of your life you choose to apply it. Simply by taking the time to educate yourself, you have grown leaps and bounds in adding to the tools that will push you forward to success.

If you were in a rut before, you now know that it is your responsibility alone to pave a new path and dig yourself out of it. You alone are responsible for cultivating your success and creating opportunities for yourself.

If you had no idea what you wanted to do with your life before, you could now use mental models like the circle of competence to put the pieces together. What are you good at? What brings you joy? What lies within your area of competence that you want to pursue?

If your relationships, romantically, familial, or friendship, were lacking, you now know about tools like personality assessments you can use to work on those relationships. Effort Is an important aspect of creating a lasting friendship, romantic relationship, or working family relationship, but if you're concentrating that effort in the wrong area, or speaking the wrong love language, your effort might be better suited elsewhere.

Finally, if you came to this book because you're just not happy anymore, you are now empowered to change your life. You know what will bring you success, but better than that, you've learned about mental toughness and stoicism. Remember that there are things outside of your control. In fact, you can't raise a finger and fix most of the world.

What you do have control over is how you choose to feel in those situations. You can allow external situations to ruin your day and your happiness, or you can take a deep breath, shrug your shoulders, and move on. You can determine your own sense of success and joy.

All of that has always been up to you. Now you just have more tools to utilize it.

# Conclusion

In this book, we learned about several different mental models:

- The First Principles mental model, famously used by Elon Musk to build rockets from scratch

- Ivan Pavlov's Classical Conditioning mental model, in which dogs salivated at the sound of a heel click and Little Albert learned to be afraid of white rats

- Scenario Analysis, a mental model that allows us to prepare for the day ahead by visualizing the challenges we might face

- The Circle of Competence mental model, used by Charlie Munger and Warren Buffet, which states that the surest way to success is defining your boundaries of competence and staying within them

- The Eisenhower Matrix, developed by the former President to assist in prioritizing task lists

- B.J. Fogg's Tiny Habits mental model, where we were inspired to create big, lasting changes by consistently meeting tiny goals

- The Commitment and Consistency Bias, where we learned that what people think of us can drive how we behave

- Cognitive Appraisal, a mental model that empowered us to decide for ourselves how to feel, and

- The Lollapalooza Effect, which states that as strong as one mental model is on its' own, a toolkit of overlapping mental models is much more powerful

You've done it. You have officially taken the first step toward being a more self-disciplined, focused, successful person with your new-found knowledge of mental models. I hope your journey won't stop here. Although this book provided a comprehensive summary of multiple mental models, there are hundreds of different models out there.

There might be a mental model that really clicks with you but wasn't covered in these chapters. You owe to yourself and your future successes to find those mental models that will work best for you.

Thank you for reading this book all the way through to the end. I hope it was an informative read and able to provide you with more tools to achieve your goals, whatever they may be.

Do you remember when you first began reading this book, and I asked you at the end of the introduction to think about your goals and what this book would do for them? Think about them now. Have they changed or adapted? Have you added onto your list of things you want to accomplish? Use the momentum you've gained by learning about mental models to make changes to your life to get there. Your habits and routines should reflect the person you want to be and the success you hope to achieve. Do they? What can you do, using the knowledge we've walked through in this book, to alter your day-to-day life to better fit the image of the person you hope to be in a year?

One tool for mental models discussed in this book briefly, but never at length, is journaling. Grabbing a notebook and making it your mission to fill it will help with every mental model, regardless of your goals. To continue the journey you started by reading this book, go out and grab a notebook. Here's what you will find when you journal about mental models:

- Writing down what you want to achieve makes your goals and habits more than just a passing thought. By physically writing down what you dream of on paper, you are making a more concrete pact to yourself to actually get it done.

- If you struggle with defining your goals, journaling using prompts can help you think through what you want to achieve and why. Don't let the word 'goal' scare you into paralysis. A goal is just a mile marker on the path to get where you ultimately want to end up. Journaling about the end game can help you to establish what those mile markers might look like.

- Writing also helps you to recognize passions you didn't know were there before. Often, writing can feel like meditation. It's a time to be totally present with your thoughts, so ideas flow out of you naturally when you're concentrating on only yourself and your future.

- By journaling, you'll realize that some mental models, like the Eisenhower Matrix, are just easier to see on paper. It's hard to keep track of lists and tasks when they're all jumbled in your head.

- Journaling can also help keep track of your gratitude habit. It's so interesting to look back after a while and see what you were grateful for back then and what you've maybe lost focus of but can reenergize now.

- Some methods of journaling, like the Bullet Journal, can also help keep you organized and become a part of your self-discipline regimen. Organized journaling can help keep track of your habits and schedule, and give an extra boost of motivation by providing a box for you to check off after a task is completed.

Finally, mental models are incredible tools, but they are just that: tools. No self-help routine or psychology trick is the magic path to success. These tools exist for you to collect and hopefully be able to put to use, but as Maya Angelou famously said, nothing will work if you don't. If you really want to see your dreams tangibly in front of you, the only person who's going to be able to make that happen is you.

You are the only person qualified to bring your goals to life. You are the only one who is excited enough and willing enough to make your future as beautiful as you've always dreamed it would be. No magic tool is going to work as well as your own grit, passion, and excitement for your dreams. This is it. The end of the line. Go get 'em, tiger.